HEADLINE HISTORY

One hundred years of Essex history from the pages of the Essex Chronicle newspaper

by Stephen Hussey

ESSEX RECORD OFFICE
PUBLICATIONS

Published by the Essex Record Office in association with the Essex Chronicle

DEDICATION

For Julia and Imogen.

Published by the
ESSEX RECORD OFFICE
Wharf Road
Chelmsford
Essex CM2 6YT

©Essex County Council, 2000

All rights reserved
This book may not be reproduced, in whole or in part, in any form, without written permission from the publishers

A catalogue record for this book
is available from the British Library

ISBN 1 898529 16 7

Essex Record Office Publication No. 142

Designed and produced by Keith Mirams
Printed in England by Lavenham Press

FOREWORD

"It has often been thought surprising that the county of Essex, which is one of the most considerable in England, should be without a newspaper, the source of information and the channel of intelligence".

These are the words William Strupar wrote 'To The Public' in the leader of the first edition of the *Chelmsford Chronicle or Essex Weekly Advertiser* published on August 10, 1764. He went on to state that the *Chronicle*, later renamed the *Essex Chronicle*, "will not be confined to articles of intelligence only, for variety of useful, instructive, and entertaining matter shall be occasionally inserted in it, so that it will not simply be a news-paper, but a repository of every kind of useful knowledge, and may not be improperly called 'THE FAMILY LIBRARY'".

Headline History is in some way continuing what William Strupar set out to achieve.

Stephen Hussey has travelled through many editions of the *Chronicle* from 1897 to gather an absorbing collection of historical chapters from the words of journalists and the views of their editors whose contemporaneous works capture a variety of events during one hundred years of publishing in Essex. Through his skill as a historian, Dr. Hussey has brought these events to life again, not only through the printed word but also interactively with the spoken word from the sound archives. While writing this book, Dr Hussey was the manager of the Essex Sound Archive at the Essex Record Office. The CD that accompanies this book includes extracts from the archives, adding a personal and a greater depth to a collection of already richly illuminated events. This spoken record of individual memories is a fascinating recollection.

Most readers will still remember much that is recalled during the latter years of the last century and will have their own visions and views. And the material from the pages of the earlier editions of the newspaper express more than just a basic historical outline. They contain a panorama of past communities; of fashions that now seem old-fashioned; of views that are perhaps no longer valid in the climate of the 21st century. But there is a magnetism contained in these pages that is not unlike finding an old newspaper and turning through the pages to discover something that is familiar or that enriches your knowledge of past events.

The Essex Record Office, where the newspapers are carefully preserved and where the Essex Sound Archive is located, has helped to bring together the ingredients for this joint publication.

Headline History sets out to be as entertaining as it is instructive and I hope you will find it a useful addition to your family library.

Stuart Rawlins
Editor, Essex Chronicle Series

CONTENTS

Foreword		iii
Contents		v
Acknowledgements		vi
Introduction		vii
1897	Diamond Jubilee	1
1901	The Death of Queen Victoria	5
1905	The Witham Rail Disaster	9
1914	The Essex Countryside in Dispute	13
1918	Influenza Epidemic	18
1926	The General Strike	23
1927	The Murder of P.C. Gutteridge	27
1930	The Depression	31
1945	War, the Final Months	36
1948	The Great Cup Run	41
1953	The Floods	46
1953	The Dawn of a New Elizabethan Age	52
1963	A Consumer Revolution	59
1964	Oh, Dr Beeching!	63
1979	Election	68
1987	The Great Storm	72
1997	The Death of Diana	78
Index		83

ACKNOWLEDGEMENTS

I am indebted to the following people, institutions and organisations for their help: Sarah Ball, June Beardsley, Ron Bond, Arthur Brown, Jenny Butler, Chelmsford Chronicle Series Ltd., Chelmsford Library, Geoff Clarke, Colchester Library, Colchester Recalled, Colchester United Football Club, Sue Cubbin, Keith Dean, East Anglian Railway Museum (Chappel), Lee Edwards, Essex Record Office, Essex Wildlife Trust, Marcel Glover, Marion Gowlett, Ken Hall, Richard Harris, Susan Harte, John Hill, Linda Jones, Susan King, Rose Marshall, Paul Mason, Keith Mirams, Andrew Phillips, Julia Rankin, Stuart Rawlins, Julian Reid, David Rees, Paula Roberts, Katharine Schofield, Maureen Scollan, Richard Shackle, Janet Smith, Andrew Tilbrook, University of Essex, Malcolm White and Geraldine Willden.

Finally, my thanks to all those who agreed to be interviewed for this project and who shared their memories of Essex's past so generously with me.

Photographic Acknowledgements:

Page 15 by kind permission of *Essex Countryside Magazine*.
Page 61 by kind permission of Rank Holidays Division Limited.

INTRODUCTION

Each chapter of this book is based upon a single event in the history of Essex. Together they represent a guide to the people and places of the county during the last one hundred years or so of the millennium. It is a history that has seen remarkable change, yet it has also witnessed the preservation of enough key elements to ensure that there remains, for many people, an unmistakable Essex identity.

The decision as to which events to include in this history and which to leave out was one that took many hours. It was an inevitable problem, for the history of Essex is one that is easy to start but tough to finish, such is its richness and diversity. There are some events that by their reputation or by their magnitude make obvious candidates for inclusion. However, there are others whose claims are less obvious, but which on closer inspection show themselves to be every bit as interesting, and every bit as important, to an understanding of the county's past.

Events such as the Diamond Jubilee of Queen Victoria in 1897 and the great flood of February 1953 are amongst those with clear-cut claims. Each stand as familiar landmarks in the history of the county, but even with these well-known events the focus taken by *Headline History* is not always so obvious. By revisiting them it is still possible to uncover new aspects in their stories and even to discover parts of their tales that have lain buried, hidden from wider view until now. For example, do you know which town in Essex scandalised its own citizens and outraged its neighbours by failing to celebrate the Queen in 1897? Do you also know that in the aftermath of the 1953 floods the police had to deploy special anti-looting squads in order to protect the unguarded homes of evacuated families from unscrupulous people who preyed on them?

Beyond these stories, other chapters tackle episodes in the county's history that have been either ignored or else overlooked by historians. For example, there is the story of how Metropolitan Police re-enforcements were called in to patrol day and night in the fields and along the lanes of Essex villages during a bitter, and sometimes violent, agricultural labourers' strike in 1914. There is the history of the brief but brutal influenza epidemic that struck with deadly force at returning soldiers and their families during the winter of 1918. There is also the remarkable tale from 1948 of how one of the county's non-league football teams reached the final stages of the F.A. Cup, of how its fans enjoyed the glory and the club's directors enjoyed the profits.

Throughout each of the chapters you will read of a history that is individual to Essex and its people. It is a history that has at times been remarkable, but at others hum-drum and mundane. One which has sometimes been triumphant and other times tragic. One that has seen vast changes but then also significant continuities.

The book draws its information from two principal sources. The first is the pages of the *Essex Chronicle*, a newspaper with its own lengthy and proud history. It was Friday 10 August 1764 when William Strupar, printer and publisher, issued the first edition of his new weekly, the *Chelmsford Chronicle, or Essex Weekly Advertiser*, as it was then called. The newspaper soon became a success. In the years before 1922, when the family ritual of listening to the wireless began to emerge, it was the *Chronicle* that kept many Essex people in touch with the wider world. The importance of the local press at this time was immense, for as readers scanned the tiny print and cramped pages of the *Chronicle*, they were linking themselves into a global news gathering system. It was true that some of this news took weeks to reach their eyes, but nonetheless there it was, in black and white, telling them of events as diverse as the American Declaration of Independence of 1776, the battle of Waterloo in 1815, the Coronation of Queen Victoria in 1837, and the opening of the Suez Canal in 1869.

The *Chronicle* went on bringing news to the county throughout the twentieth century. Now, as we look back, it represents a marvellous, self-contained archive for Essex's history. In the course of researching and writing this book I have had to read a good deal of the last one hundred years of the newspaper. With every turn of its yellowing pages, with every glance at its headlines and news stories, the *Chronicle* yielded fascinating information. Nevertheless, we need to be careful with newspapers, for they can never represent a mirror image of the past, a literal documentation of times gone. When reading them we need to remind ourselves that press reporting does not produce a neutral record. Instead, what we read years later is an image of the past controlled by a set of intertwined influences. Ultimately any edition of a newspaper is the product of its own times and reflects the morality, opinions, behaviour, fashions and fads of the day. We need to recognize, too, that the words we read come from the pens of individual journalists, whose work was in turn read and redrafted by their editors. Each held their own views and had their own axes to grind, just like the historians of today. Newspapers also have proprietors whose ultimate aim is to sell more of their product and who can be ruthless in their drive to do so.

As a consequence *Headline History* cannot make the claim to be a faithful factual account of events over the last one hundred years. But, rather than despair with the inaccuracies and biases of the press, we can, with a little imagination, use them to our own ends, producing a history that is richer still. From every outraged editorial, every letter of complaint from a reader, every advertisement promising a miracle product, every banner headline, we can learn a little more of the ways in which the people of Essex thought, felt and expressed their opinions.

The second source for this book are the people of Essex themselves. Inside the front cover you will find a CD. This has been compiled from the archives of the Essex Sound Archive, which forms part of the Essex Record Office, the storehouse of the county's heritage. The Archive contains the voices and memories of hundreds of people who have witnessed Essex history at first hand. Your CD is a small selection of these, but it adds an extra dimension to the book. For example, it allows you to hear the voice of one of the more fortunate victims of the 1918 flu epidemic, and the memories of the footballer who played against the great Stanley Matthews in 1948, and of survivors of the great flood in 1953. Some of the recordings are now very old; even so, what some might lack in sound quality they more than make up for in the fascinating and sometimes unique detail that they give us. After all, when you play this CD you are literally listening to the sound of the county's past. So sit back, read the book, and listen to Essex as it speaks to you.

Using the CD:
Where you see this symbol 回 at the end of a chapter you have the opportunity to listen to the voices of Essex people recalling their experiences of the event concerned. You will see that the symbol is followed by a number, and this refers to the track number on the CD. Select that number on your CD player to hear the appropriate sound excerpt.

We start the story, not in the twentieth century, but in June 1897. Victoria had come to the throne sixty years previously and the celebrations to mark this unique milestone were widespread and enthusiastic. Villagers and townspeople of Essex, as elsewhere, took an opportunity to mark not only their aged monarch's Diamond Jubilee but also the belief that Britain, with its huge empire, stood at the world's zenith...

1897 THE DIAMOND JUBILEE: 'a capital festivity'

BY THE TIME of her Diamond Jubilee Victoria had reigned longer than any other British monarch. Her sovereignty had also coincided with the high-point of the nation's power overseas. By 1897 Victoria was the living representation of this command. Yet the Queen had not enjoyed unbroken popularity. Her ten year self-imposed seclusion after the death of her husband Prince Albert in 1861, and the rumours of an intimate relationship with her Scottish confidant John Brown, had not always endeared her to the public.

However, the Jubilee did seem to succeed in bringing much of the nation together in celebration. Amongst the extensive number of column inches devoted by the *Essex County Chronicle* (as it was then known) to the festivities, it is possible to find reports of events from almost every corner of Essex. Above all else these showed a genuine and widespread affection towards the Queen. At Halstead, for example, the paper reported that *'every creed and class joined together, the result was all that could be desired'*. While at Galleywood it was said that *'the festivities went as merrily as a marriage bell'*, although it was perhaps with a touch of over-excitement that the report from Great Baddow read *'The day was one of the happiest ever spent by the inhabitants'*. Perhaps it was the opportunity for a display of patriotism that inspired people. Perhaps it was also Victoria herself. As a widow and mother to nine children she personified the values of the family that the Victorian age had come to embrace, at least on its surface. But the celebrations also owed something to the growth of the mass media, of which regional newspapers such as the *Chronicle* were a vital part. People, even in the remotest parts of the countryside, now knew a good deal about their monarch. They knew what she looked like, they read of her royal engagements, the decisions of her government and the progress of her empire. Victoria was in part the property of her people and the Diamond Jubilee festivities reflected this.

THE LONDON SCENE

Amongst the nation-wide celebrations the grandest were in London where a large military procession, including 30,000 troops drawn from across the empire, escorted the Queen to a service at St. Paul's Cathedral. The crowds included Essex men and women who the *Chronicle* reported had travelled *'chiefly between the ghostly hours of one and six in the morning'* to enjoy

THE DIAMOND JUBILEE.
ROYAL PROCESSION IN LONDON.
A SCENE OF UNPARALLELED SPLENDOUR.
THE JUBILEE PORTRAIT OF THE QUEEN.

Street celebrations: here the people of Witham enjoy the Jubilee

the spectacle. Elsewhere 3,000 beacons were lit upon *'the loftiest hills in the kingdom...from Orkney to a solitary fire on the French coast'*.

In Essex many communities had been planning their own celebrations for months. Committees had been formed, subscriptions taken and programmes formulated. The plans did not always proceed smoothly, as the newspaper commented: *'some preliminary discussions about the Jubilee, or the arrangements made for it, led to more or less discontent'*. Nevertheless Jubilee day, Tuesday 22nd June, was bright and warm. For most people it was also a holiday, and one that they meant to enjoy in a variety of ways. In fact the most startling feature of the day was to be the diversity in the celebrations.

HILL-TOP BEACONS

Some communities chose to contribute to the national display of hill-top beacons. Taking advantage of its elevated position, Danbury's fire was said to be amongst the most impressive of all and was *'pointed to by thousands all over Essex who espied the flames as they shot high into the heavens'*. At Pleshey the fire was more dramatic still but only because a stray spark had ignited the thatch of two adjoining cottages, destroying them both.

Time and food were recurring themes in other celebrations. Both Billericay and Brentwood rejoiced with the unveiling of new or renewed town clocks. Many places held feasts. Sometimes these were restricted to the children and elderly. But elsewhere whole communities seem to have sat down together to eat. At Steeple Bumpstead this involved the consumption of what was described as *'a monster meat tea'*, after which some brave villagers were still able to take part in *'senior sports'*. Even the residents of Essex's workhouses were treated, although as the *Chronicle* commented with a degree of sarcasm *'No genius has arisen among the [poor law] guardians equal to devising anything more suitable than roast beef and plum pudding even on a hot mid-summer's day'*. Elsewhere other communities looked to give their residents more longer-lasting tributes to their Queen. At Burnham-on-Crouch, for example, a subscription of £75 had enabled the minting of commemorative medals for townspeople.

Brilliant weather favoured the celebration of the sixtieth year of the good Queen VICTORIA's reign. There is hardly a parish in Essex, however small, in which some form of rejoicing did not take place. Almost everywhere we hear of processions, decorations, and festive dinners and teas, with a display of fireworks or a bonfire to end up with. It is pleasant to think that in these arrangements the poor, the aged, the school children, and those generally who have little to cheer them during the year, were especially provided for. There were little hitches, a disagreement here and there, as our reports show, but on the whole happiness without alloy distinguished the festivities, and the day was one to which QUEEN and people will long look back with emotions of pride and pleasure.

PROCESSIONS

However, it was through the holding of processions that most chose to celebrate. Some of these were modest, like the one at Tollesbury where ***'a floral rally of adorned mail carts and perambulators'*** was led by children carrying a banner which read ***'The babies of Tollesbury send their greetings to their Queen'***. Some seem slightly bizarre, such as the parade of decorated bicycles in Colchester, the first prize for which was won by a tandem ***'fitted up as a complete representation of HMS Royal Sovereign'***. Others were large undertakings, like the ***'miscellaneous and well-organised procession'*** held in Braintree which was said to stretch for over three-quarters of a mile in length. Here, as elsewhere, streets were bedecked with decorations and illuminations, which in Braintree's case were so fine ***'that people were loth to go to bed, many staying out all night admiring them'***.

Wherever one went in the county, wherever a Diamond Jubilee celebration was held, there was also the accompaniment of a strong scent of competition. Festivities gave towns an ideal chance to show off their municipal pride and worth. Coggeshall, for example, claimed that its street decorations and lights had ***'put those of most surrounding parishes entirely in the shade'***, while Braintree proclaimed its own efforts as ***'a credit to the town's loyalty and a pattern to some other larger places'***.

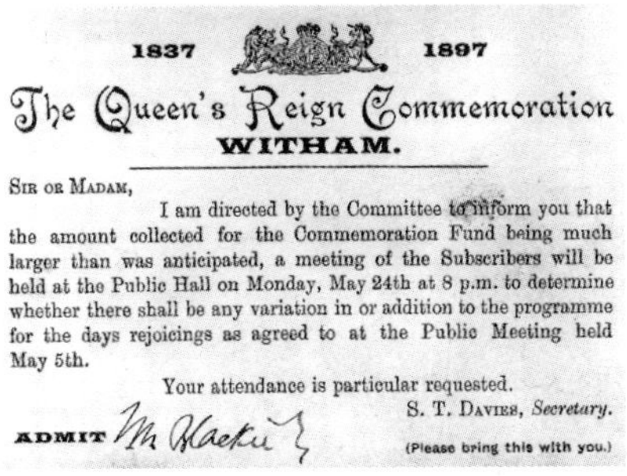

1837 1897

The Queen's Reign Commemoration

WITHAM.

SIR OR MADAM,

I am directed by the Committee to inform you that the amount collected for the Commemoration Fund being much larger than was anticipated, a meeting of the Subscribers will be held at the Public Hall on Monday, May 24th at 8 p.m. to determine whether there shall be any variation in or addition to the programme for the days rejoicings as agreed to at the Public Meeting held May 5th.

Your attendance is particular requested.

S. T. DAVIES, *Secretary.*

ADMIT

(Please bring this with you.)

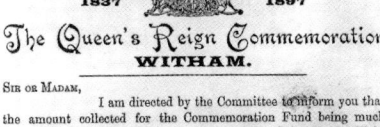

1897 saw scores of Commemoration Committees founded. Fund raising and the distribution of funds were their central task, as this communication from the Witham Committee indicates

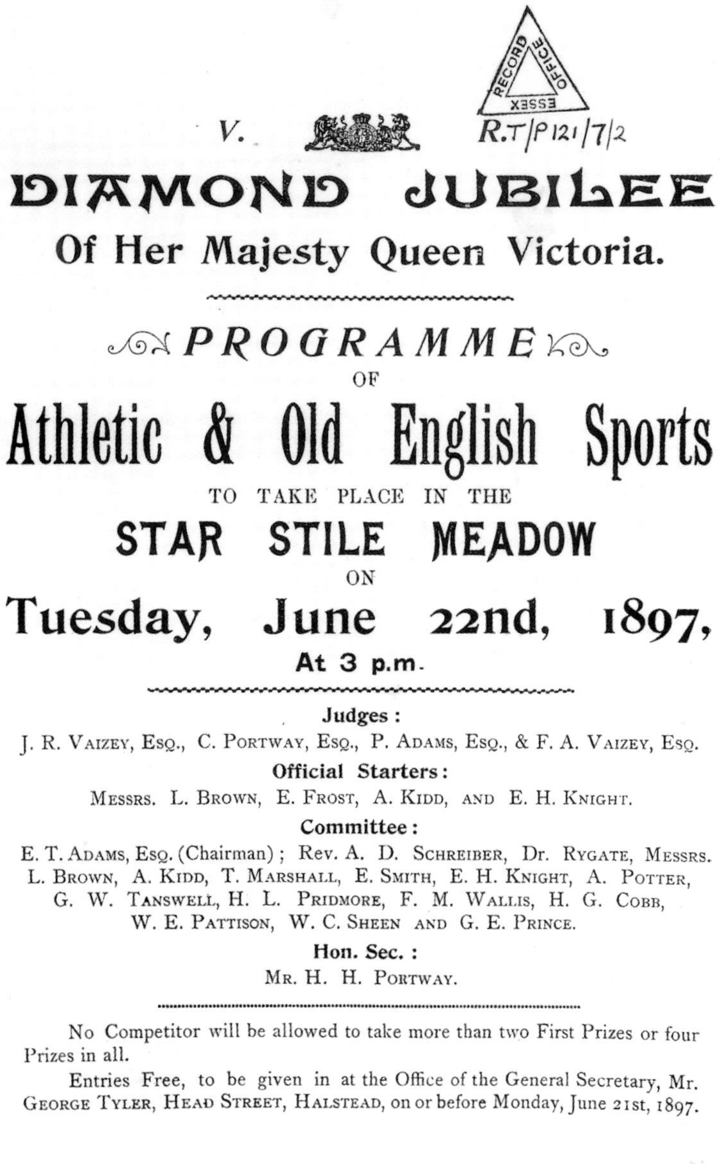

V. R.T/P121/7/2

ESSEX RECORD OFFICE

DIAMOND JUBILEE

Of Her Majesty Queen Victoria.

PROGRAMME

OF

Athletic & Old English Sports

TO TAKE PLACE IN THE

STAR STILE MEADOW

ON

Tuesday, June 22nd, 1897,

At 3 p.m.

Judges:

J. R. VAIZEY, ESQ., C. PORTWAY, ESQ., P. ADAMS, ESQ., & F. A. VAIZEY, ESQ.

Official Starters:

MESSRS. L. BROWN, E. FROST, A. KIDD, AND E. H. KNIGHT.

Committee:

E. T. ADAMS, ESQ. (Chairman); REV. A. D. SCHREIBER, DR. RYGATE, MESSRS. L. BROWN, A. KIDD, T. MARSHALL, E. SMITH, E. H. KNIGHT, A. POTTER, G. W. TANSWELL, H. L. PRIDMORE, F. M. WALLIS, H. G. COBB, W. E. PATTISON, W. C. SHEEN AND G. E. PRINCE.

Hon. Sec.:

MR. H. H. PORTWAY.

No Competitor will be allowed to take more than two First Prizes or four Prizes in all.

Entries Free, to be given in at the Office of the General Secretary, Mr. GEORGE TYLER, HEAD STREET, HALSTEAD, on or before Monday, June 21st, 1897.

Halstead marked the Diamond Jubilee in energetic fashion

Braintree's comments might well have been aimed at communities like that at Stanford Rivers, near Ongar, where villagers hung out black flags in protest that no suitable celebration had been arranged. Or at Wickford, where the absence of celebrations caused the *Chronicle* to describe the streets as **'deserted'** as **'all the inhabitants had gone to other places and no one was to be seen'**, all this despite the village containing **'several wealthy freeholders to whom money is no object'**. But it was Chelmsford, the county town, that proved most lacklustre in its efforts. The newspaper describes its streets as being **'not very liberally decorated'**, while the main form of entertainment for the townspeople was a Punch and Judy show at total expenditure of just £8. This appears to have proved too little for some:

'In the afternoon a resourceful gentleman upon whom the attraction of the Punch and Judy show had begun to pall, gave vent to his feelings by informing those about him that "This ain't no bloomin' good! I could make more fun myself". He was as good as his word. Divesting himself of his coat only, he proceeded to the river bank, and, after some time, swam off the effects of his disgust.'

Others used Chelmsford's poor effort as an opportunity to demonstrate their anger at the town's council and Jubilee Committee in more dramatic fashion. Carrying a mock coffin, dressed in black and bearing a banner which read **'CHELMSFORD IS DEAD'** a crowd of protesters paraded the town's streets chanting funeral dirges to the accompaniment of a concertina.

A TEMPEST

But if the Diamond Jubilee celebrations had been lacklustre in Chelmsford, they were to be short-lived in many other Essex towns and villages. Two days later, in what was one of the most dramatic weeks in the history of the county, the heart of Essex was hit by a devastating storm. From Ongar through Chelmsford to Kelvedon, Maldon and Brightlingsea, a central band of the county witnessed winds, hailstones and lightning of such intensity that the *Chronicle* estimated that **'a tempest of such terrific force, attended by so much havoc and destruction has certainly never occurred in Essex before'**. The cries and shrieks of people caught outdoors in the storm were said to be **'terrible'** as **'they were mercilessly beaten by the hailstones'**. Houses had windows and even roofs penetrated by their force. At Great Baddow it was even reported that 200 partridges and pheasants had been killed by the hail, **'cut as if they had been struck by a bullet'**.

CRUEL TWIST

Yet it was agriculture, still the staple industry of the county and its biggest employer, that felt the worst of the storm. Crops which at 2pm on the Thursday afternoon had **'stood green and smiling'**, by 3pm **'had been ruthlessly cut down and beaten into almost indistinguishable pulp and shreds'**. For farmers whose farms had been barely profitable since the 1870s the storm was a cruel twist of fate. For the long suffering and underpaid farm labourer it presented more immediate problems, for as the *Chronicle* warned:

'It must not be forgotten that this calamity will seriously affect the labouring class in the districts where it has occurred. If there be little or no harvest, there will be little or no work for the labouring man, and this is at a time of year when he is accustomed to get a few pounds together for the payment of his rent and the purchase of clothing for his family.'

For this portion of the Essex population, the celebrations of the Diamond Jubilee must have seemed just a fleeting diversion from a never-ending struggle.

THE TORNADO IN ESSEX.

FIRST ACCOUNTS PALE INTO INSIGNIFICANCE.

WHOLE FARMS SWEPT CLEAN OF CROPS.

ENORMOUS DESTRUCTION OF VEGETABLES AND FRUIT.

HAILSTONES BIGGER THAN HENS' EGGS.

SLATES AND IRON ROOFS PENETRATED.

No artist in words, however graphic his powers, could paint an adequate picture of the cyclone or tornado which devastated a large portion of the county of Essex on Midsummerday. Most people, when they read on Friday morning of the terrific fury of the blast, of the continuous thunder and lightning, of the driving sheets of rain, of the fall of tons of hailstones, many of them larger than walnuts, and of the havoc wrought among farm and garden crops and among houses and other buildings, would doubtless leap to the conclusion that newspaper writers, in the excitement of the moment, had greatly over-coloured the canvas. The fact, alas, is the other way about. All the details that have come to hand since the first accounts were published show that there was not a trait which might not have been enlarged. This fearful storm turns out to have been a complete catastrophe. From Epping in the west of the county to Burnham and Clacton in the east, and though a considerable belt of the county from north to south, the havoc was tremendous and incalculable. Probably there are not less than a hundred square miles of the county where the hope of a harvest has been practically destroyed.

The scale of celebrations for the Diamond Jubilee of 1897 had shown the pride with which Essex viewed its Queen and country. Although not unexpected, her death in the first weeks of 1901 came swiftly and seemed to shake the confidence of the nation. The Victorian age was over, a new century and a new era lay ahead. Both were tinged with uncertainty...

1901 THE DEATH OF QUEEN VICTORIA: 'tears of the greatest grief'

GIVEN THAT OUR our own marking of the new millennium occurred in the year 2000, it is interesting to note that the Victorians chose 1901 and not 1900 as the year in which to welcome their entrance into the twentieth century. Even so, 1st January 1901 seems to have stirred few Essex imaginations. Perhaps it was the recent outbreak of the deadly disease anthrax in the county's cattle farms that preoccupied people's thoughts, or perhaps it was the poor weather that greeted the new year that dampened people's spirits. Whatever the reason, there were few celebrations and certainly nothing to compare with the Diamond Jubilee of four years previously.

THE NEW AGE
Only at church and in chapel was the occasion marked consistently. But even here many of the services were notable less for their mood of celebration than for expressions of doubt about the direction the new age might take. In his annual New Year address the Bishop of Colchester seemed to capture this feeling. As the *Essex County Chronicle* remarked **'He thanked God for a Queen who was the Lord's minister. In granting her a long life "He hath been mindful of us". They rejoiced in the Queen and her beneficent rule, for example, her character, her sympathy, but they recognised it as the working of God's grace - the mark of God's love to this nation.'** The Bishop then looked back over the Queen's reign where all seemed reassuring. **'There had been a great advance in scientific knowledge, facility of locomotion by the sea and land, facility of communication by post, telegraph, and telephone, increase in luxury for the prosperous, and of the necessaries of life for the poor.'** Yet he also warned of stark difficulties that remained; **'the distance between extremes of wealth and poverty was still great indeed, and was fraught with danger for the community. Had wars ceased? Was slavery abolished? Was intemperance checked? Was faith found on the earth? Was the world being converted? These questions could not be accurately answered'.**

Doubt was well-founded, for while other nations might marvel at Victorian Britain's power and wealth, the nation contained its own growing problems and insecurities. The Boer war in South Africa (1899-1902) was to take the lives of 5,000 British soldiers and showed that imperial ambition came only at

Heavy black printed borders marked the Essex Chronicle's coverage of the Queen's death

DEATH OF THE QUEEN.

PEACEFUL CLOSE OF A MEMORABLE REIGN

The long, memorable, and beneficent reign of our revered Sovereign, Queen Victoria, came to a close on Tuesday last, the 22nd inst., when Her Majesty died, at half-past six in the evening, surrounded by her children and grandchildren, at Osborne House, Isle of Wight.

The first official intimation of the mournful event was a telegram from the Prince of Wales to the Lord Mayor, dated Osborne, 6.45 p.m.:— "My beloved mother, the Queen, has just passed away, surrounded by her children and grandchildren.—Albert Edward."

The bulletins issued in the earlier part of the day had foreshadowed a fatal termination to her Majesty's illness. At eight a.m. the physicians announced that the Queen showed signs of diminishing strength, and that her Majesty's condition had again assumed a serious aspect. At noon there was favourable bulletin, stating change for the worse in the She had recognized the Royal family wh asleep. At fou announcemen sinking, an

a price. Closer to hand the struggle for 'Home Rule' from Irish nationalists continued to rumble on, while the late nineteenth century had also seen growing tensions spreading along class lines. By 1901 manual workers numbered fourteen million out of the nation's eighteen million workforce, a growing number were now represented by trade unions, most men now had the vote and some looked to the socialist Independent Labour Party to represent them. In addition to this, cracks in the power of Britain's economy were beginning to show as competition from North America, Australasia and Europe started to wear away at the nation's economic pre-eminence.

UNCERTAIN FUTURES

Then on 22nd January 1901 came the news that the Queen was dead, and with her went a central source of the country's continuity and stability. The path ahead now began to look uncertain.

The Queen's death also highlighted what had perhaps been the biggest change to have come over British life during her long reign: the development of rapid mass-communication. It was Tuesday at 6.30pm when Victoria died in her bed chamber at Osborne House on the Isle of Wight. Just 30 minutes later the news was already being talked of in Essex's towns and villages. By the Friday of the same week, the county's newspapers were full of news relating to the Queen's passing, including not only reaction from at home, but from every part of Britain's far-flung empire.

The *Chronicle*'s own coverage was extensive, the newspaper marking the occasion with heavy black lines between its columns. Coming under the simple headline *'Death of the Queen'* its tone was unfailingly loyal and reverential:

'A life which has been of priceless value to the British Empire, and, indeed to nearly every part of the world, came to an end on Tuesday evening, when at half-past six o'clock the great and good QUEEN VICTORIA breathed her last. It is hardly too much to say that the event has cast a Universe into mourning. Everybody loved, and had cause to love, a Sovereign in whom gentleness and fitness for a lofty position were united in such an extraordinary degree. Her Majesty was so good as wife, widow, mother and sovereign, that every one of us could have wished that she might be exempted from the common lot of mortality.'

Around the county people went into mourning. The *Chronicle* wrote of the population shedding *'tears in the greatest grief that the nation has ever known'*, and that *'there appeared a visible shadow on the faces of the people'*. At Great Dunmow, it was said, *'The Queen's death caused a painful sensation'*. At Halstead *'the profoundest regret was visible'*. At Maldon, it was reported, *'signs of mourning are everywhere'*. While at Tillingham the correspondent recorded simply that *'Only one sentiment, that of loss, seems to pervade all men'*. Throughout Essex shops and businesses put up black shutters, policemen wore black crepe armbands and black ties were much in evidence on men, with mourning dress for women. At Harwich ships in the harbour flew their flags at half-mast, while the anchored *HMS Severn* fired its minute guns in sombre salute. Everywhere church bells were muffled and then rung slowly, calling church-goers to memorial services.

Only at Witham were there signs of deviance from this solemn pattern. Here the news of the Queen's death reached the town just as the annual Tradesman's Ball was beginning and, rather than postponing proceedings, the revellers continued to enjoy the food, drink and music laid before them. This display of ostentatious celebration in the face of such news brought damning condemnation from the *Chronicle*'s own editorial:

'We are sorry to hear that though the sad news was known in the room in

1901 THE DEATH OF QUEEN VICTORIA

the early evening, the dancing was continued till the usual hour. It is difficult to understand how loyal English people could be so indifferent to a sorrow that was moving, not only a nation, but an empire. Their conduct has caused much indignation in the town. Rich and poor alike condemn it, and marvel at the thoughtless behaviour of presumably well-educated people.'

It seems that there was to be no event, however grave, that could prevent the people of Witham from enjoying themselves that night.

That was the time when...

As sad as the death of Queen Victoria was, it did have benefits for some in the county. The day of the Queen's funeral and the weeks that followed brought many into local shops seeking out the mourning clothes that Victoria had made her own trademark. *'NATIONAL MOURNING, NATIONAL MOURNING'* ran the advertising headline of J.J. Crowe and Co. Ltd. of Brentwood. *'Every requisite in both Ladies and Gentlemen's wear for the proper observance of the Great Calamity that has befallen the nation.'*

In Chelmsford Bolingbroke were advertising their annual winter sale on the promise of *'General Mourning at Reduced Prices: Black costumes, coats and skirts, black shawls and wraps, black ties and scarves, black goods and lace goods, black and complementary millinery'*. The store also promised that *'Notwithstanding the unprecedented demand for Mourning Apparel, our numerous Patrons may rely upon our best endeavours to execute their valued orders with the utmost despatch'*.

Colchester people gather in the town's High Street to hear news of Queen Victoria's succession by Edward VII

Source: Philip Giffon, Colchester

At this time the *Chronicle* carried many advertisements for new and novel goods and services. Most of them were never to find a secure market, but occasionally it is possible to see a product that was to meet with success, heralding a new period for the consumer. Take for example this early advertisement for frozen foods: *'ICES! ICES! - As supplied by us to the great Steamship Companies, Theatres, and Aristocracy. Ices and Ice puddings sent any distance in brick shape, or cut into small cakes. Many flavours. Will keep solid for 12 hours. Charges moderate - Horton Ices'*.

In 1901 the *Chronicle*'s sports column was written by the aptly named *'Kickett Forward'*. Although his writing was mostly a genteel comment on the results and performances of the past week, it did occasionally pass judgement on less savoury sporting episodes. January contained a report of an incident at a football match in Colchester between the Royal Artillery and the Mid-Week Club. Here a dispute had arisen around *'the non-use of goal nets and the non-roping off of the ground'*. The unfortunate referee, Mr Hicks, was *'vigorously hooted, while at the close a crowd of almost 100 - chiefly civilians - surrounded and mobbed him, some threatening to strike him. Stones were thrown and one of these struck Mr Hicks on the head, but he fortunately received no serious injury'*. Hooligans at football matches, it seems, were already well-established.

Since their appearance in the middle of the nineteenth century the railways had done much to 'shrink' Essex and the world beyond. Concepts of time and distance had been altered. But however remarkable this transformation had been, for most people in 1905 the railway had become just 'ordinary'. A fixture of modern living that many used to travel to work, to school, to shop and for recreation. For them it was just another quick, cheap, reliable and safe part of life. But at 10.29 am on 1st September, in what was to be the worst train accident ever witnessed in the county, this confidence was dealt a tragic blow...

1905 THE WITHAM RAIL DISASTER: 'an indescribable scene'

THE REPORTS IN the *Essex County Chronicle* concerning the Witham rail disaster tell us as much about the local press as they do about the tragedy of the episode itself. As we will see, the tone of the reporting was graphic, even sensationalist (although the newspaper denied this at the time). The level of detail of its reports, particularly those concerning the type and extent of the victims' injuries, are something that newspapers might well shy away from today. Part of the reason for this was the stiff competition faced by local weeklies, such as the *Chronicle*, from national newspapers (a reason that the *Chronicle* itself alludes to). But the level of written description was also a symptom of the absence of photographic illustrations, which did not become a regular part of the newspaper until the inter-war years. But photographs do exist, for the pictures shown here are from local photographers who seem to have been quickly on the scene.

LUCKY ESCAPE

There was nothing with which to predict the disaster to come when the 9.27 am Great Eastern Railway express departed London Liverpool Street on-time, bound for Cromer on the north Norfolk coast. The locomotive was carrying 200 passengers in its first, second and third class carriages. Most were travelling to enjoy a late summer holiday by the sea. The express was progressing well when it made its scheduled stop, on time, in Chelmsford at 10.17am. It was here that, as the *Chronicle* later reported, **'a man running for the train just missed it'**. For this one individual this was to be a lucky escape.

From Chelmsford the train was due to make its next stop at Colchester. As it approached Witham station it was said to be **'running smoothly and exactly to time, at a rate of fifty miles an hour'**. But it was now that tragedy struck.

As the train was about to pass the approaching platforms the fourth

---

WRECK OF CROMER EXPRESS
AT WITHAM.
Taken Directly after the Accident.

PHOTOGRAPHS (12 various): 1s., 1s. 6d., and 2s. each. Packing and Postage 3d.
POSTCARDS (6 various): 12 for 1s. Postage 1d.

Can be had of
FRED. SPALDING, Photographer, Chelmsford.

The Trade Supplied.

Essex people's thirst for news provided a ready market for photographers such as Chelmsford's Fred Spalding

10 HEADLINE HISTORY

Police and railway officials survey the wreckage

carriage and those that followed it became derailed, or as the train's driver later described, **'they jumped the metals'**. The results were devastating, the train splitting into two sections. The first section, consisting of the engine and three carriages, continued through the station. The engine escaped largely unscathed. But the carriages were overturned, with the gas, which was still used to light and heat them, bursting into flame. However, it was further up the track that the scene was still more terrible. **'Of the other part of the train, consisting of eleven carriages there is a terrible tale of tragedy to record.'** Here the derailment had forced some of the carriages to mount the station platform, ploughing into the station buildings.

EYE WITNESS ACCOUNTS

The descriptions given by passengers were vivid. A boy of sixteen told the *Chronicle* that the first signs of trouble were when he felt his carriage **'kick a bit, like a kicking horse'**. It was then that he saw **'pieces of wood flash past the carriage window like cinematograph pictures'**. Another spoke of being **'bounced about like an india-rubber ball'**. While Mr Faulkner, a commercial traveller from London, told of how **'Our carriage was smashed into matchwood. I attribute my safety to having the presence of mind to fall to the floor. My clothes were torn to ribbons. I think my tall hat saved my head, but I never saw the hat again'**.

Others did not have such a lucky escape. One carriage in particular had turned on to its roof, a combination of the impact and the weight of its undercarriage crushing the compartments. It was here that the picture was said to have **'caused the bravest hearts to momentarily shrink and shudder'**, with those inside having **'met with a fearful death, or were shockingly maimed. Some were dead, some were dying, and it was very difficult to reach them.'**

Within three minutes the news of the crash had spread back along the line to Liverpool Street. The response was immediate, as a special train of doctors and railway company officials was hastily dispatched. In Witham **'great excitement prevailed in the streets; tradesmen rushed from their premises, shops were deserted, and there was a general move towards the station'**. Local doctors Karl, Edward and Gimson were summoned from their surgery as **'bandages, cotton wool and other appliances'** were thrown into their awaiting car. At the scene onlookers attempted to rescue the survivors, but as one eyewitness reported, **'It was an indescribable scene. Bodies could be observed in different parts of the wreckage, but we could not tell whether** *they were dead or alive.'* Carriage doors were pulled from the wreck and used as stretchers. The station's waiting room was hurriedly deployed as a field hospital, while the town's Corn Exchange doubled as both a reception centre for the injured and a mortuary, *'a curtain of sacking dividing the dead from the living'*.

LIVES LOST

The accident had taken the lives of eleven people. Ten died at the scene, a further victim lingering until the following morning. The dead included two spinster sisters on their way to the coast, a farmer's wife travelling with her husband and children, a travelling salesman, a Swiss national about to begin a new job in domestic service and a young man returning from Paris to his Suffolk home for the first time in four years in order to comfort his dying mother. Also killed was railway porter Joe Doole, buried beneath the platform building in which he sat eating his lunch. Alongside the dead, sixty-six passengers also suffered injuries of varying degrees.

Events moved swiftly after the accident. By the next morning new track had been laid on one of the two lines at the station and a train service was again running. At the same time the coroner's court had assembled a jury of fifteen men who were now being escorted around the crash scene, attempting to provide an explanation for the disaster. They were met with an eerie sight as **'unmistakable signs of the tragedy were apparent. The broken woodwork was stained with blood, fragments of glass, similarly stained, were scattered about the ruins, and here and there were portions of clothing. Protruding from the top was a lady's brown straw hat, crushed flat, with pink roses fastened in it, and in another part a lady's black hat was showing, together with portions of a bodice. Farther on, a book, several newspapers, a cigarette tin, a couple of dolls, and a child's broken sand shovel gave indication of the destruction of the previous morning'**.

MORBID FASCINATION

A morbid fascination with the accident grew. Even as the *Chronicle*'s correspondent returned to Chelmsford from Witham on the evening of the crash, he reported passing 258 cyclists passing in the opposite direction, all keen to witness the scene. A local policeman claimed that in one hour alone

Blood on the tracks: a derailed carriage lies amidst the broken building of Witham Station

over one hundred cyclists had stopped to view the station. By Sunday it was said that *'the scene of the disaster was visited by immense crowds of people, who came from the country roundabout by all kinds of vehicles'*. By the following Friday newspapers were carrying a prominent advert from Chelmsford photographer Fred Spalding advertising photographs and postcards *'taken directly after the accident'*.

THE BITTEREST GRIEF

The *Chronicle* itself seems to have used the crash to further its own cause. Worried by the growing competition from national newspapers, such as the Daily Mail and Daily Herald, the *Chronicle* used its coverage to take a swipe at what it termed the *'new journalism of the London papers'*. These it claimed had reported the crash using *'mere sensationalism, with too little regard either to facts or to the feelings of people who are suffering the bitterest grief'*. Alongside this condemnation it added a thinly concealed plea to bolster its own sales: *'It is hoped, after what we have recently seen and experienced, that the public will be a little more loyal than they have been to the sober press of their own county, which has honourably given a wide berth to the evil policy of piling up a worthless circulation by the administration of hourly shocks to its readers.'*

THE MEMORY REMAINS?

The cause of the crash itself was never fully established. Both the coroner's court and a later investigation by the Board of Trade proved inconclusive, although both suggested that the most likely reason lay in work to the track being done that morning. For the people who lost relatives the disaster remained with them. For Witham too, the memory of that day remained, although the new station built in 1907 must have done much to remove any visual reminders. For the wider county the tragedy held the attention of the local press for two weeks and then disappeared. Normal life resumed. Train travel was now an irreplaceable part of the modern world. A week after the disaster the *Essex County Chronicle* was carrying notices from the Great Eastern Railway on its front page. Was this an expression of condolence to the families of the dead? An apology to its customers? No. Instead it was an advertisement for cheap-day excursions to the Norfolk coast.

APPALLING RAILWAY ACCIDENT AT WITHAM.

TEN PASSENGERS KILLED AND MANY INJURED.

PATHETIC SCENES AND INCIDENTS.

OPENING OF THE INQUEST

PROGRESS OF THE INJURED.

HOW THE SIGNALMAN AVERTED FURTHER CALAMITY.

GRACIOUS MESSAGE FROM THE QUEEN.

An appalling accident to a fast through down train occurred at Witham railway station on Friday morning, in which ten persons (nine passengers and a foreman porter) were killed and 50 injured, some dangerously. The ill-fated train was the one leaving Liverpool-street at 9.27 a.m. for Felixstowe and Cromer. It stopped, as usual, at Chelmsford at 10.17, and then had a fast run before it to Colchester, but at Witham it left the metals, and, mounting the platform, smashed some of the station

By 1914, with the expansion of leisure pursuits such as hiking and cycling, the Essex countryside was being used increasingly as a place of leisure and recreation. The growing numbers of motor cars and charabancs on the county's roads opened up its interior still further, building on the work of the railways. These day-trippers, weekend cottagers and holiday makers came in search of a piece of 'traditional' England with its world of tranquillity, simplicity and stability. However, there was another side to the Essex countryside which was less harmonious and which offered the potential for trouble. In the summer of 1914 it was this side that made itself known with dramatic effect...

1914 THE ESSEX COUNTRYSIDE IN DISPUTE: 'trouble in the fields'

THE VILLAGE OF Helions Bumpstead lies close to that corner of Essex which meets Suffolk and Cambridgeshire. Today it straggles along a number of minor roads. It is small, tucked out of the way and, above all, quiet. But in October 1913 it helped to set in train a series of events that were to divide its own people and those of the surrounding communities. These were to make headlines that shocked the readers of the *Essex County Chronicle* and even occasioned questions in the House of Commons. Over the coming months there was to be a bitter strike, confrontation, arson, the involvement of Metropolitan Police reinforcements, arrests and imprisonment. All this in the heart of what was supposed to be England's 'green and pleasant land'.

TRADE UNIONS
In that October a meeting of the village's agricultural labourers voted to form a branch of the National Agricultural Labourers and Rural Workers Union. Trade unionism in the countryside was not a new phenomenon. The 1870s had seen union membership spread rapidly in rural England. This had culminated in a large-scale dispute with farmers in 1874. However, after these heady early years the trade union had dwindled and by the mid 1890s was extinct. By 1913 it had been twenty years since trade unions had existed on an Essex farm. So when news spread that within two weeks of its formation the Helions Bumpstead branch had grown to sixty members, local farmers began to show some concern. This was fuelled in early 1914 by the coming together of other men forming new branches at nearby Steeple Bumpstead, Wimbish, Birdbrook and Ashdon.

No immediate action was taken by the branches, no strikes called, no work to rule, no walk-outs. Yet their very presence was too much for some. Richard Ruffle, who farmed Copy Farm, Helions Bumpstead, was the first to move

Women workers 'stooking' sheaves at Great Waltham during World War One

against the men. In late February he issued an ultimatum to ten of his workers: either they should leave the union or he would sack them. Ruffle admitted to the press *'No demands of any kind have been made by the men. I am acting entirely on my own initiative and intend to have nothing to do with the union men on my farm.'* But his words came with another warning, for Ruffle, like many other farmers, not only employed the men but also owned the houses they and their families lived in. *'I have not given them notice to quit their houses at the moment but if they do not make up their minds soon I shall give them notice to leave the cottages which I own.'* He added *'I have nothing against the men personally'*.

Local farmers quickly copied Ruffle's response, so that within weeks much of Helions Bumpstead's agricultural labour force had effectively been locked out by their employers. However, rather than forcing the men into submission this seems to have strengthened the union. On 3rd March a meeting at the Moot Hall in Steeple Bumpstead inspired a further fifty labourers to join local branches. Two days later the *Essex County Chronicle* reported a well-attended meeting having taken place outside the Marquis of Granby pub in Helions Bumpstead. Here the crowd was addressed by union leaders and the event ended with a torchlight procession through the village.

STRIKE BALLOTS

Such was the growing confidence of the union that in early June it decided to hold strike ballots amongst all of its local branches. The results of these were overwhelming and positive. On the clear summer evening of Sunday 14th June trade union officials began touring north-west Essex telling of the decision to strike. *'They set out at midnight, waking up village after village with the loud blast of a harvest horn, a dinner bell and a lot of bicycle bells. Men, women and children came streaming out in their night attire. They received the news with much enthusiasm, bands of men, women and children parading the lanes all night long.*

The demands of the strikers were straightforward; they wished for a wage rise from thirteen to sixteen shillings a week. In addition to this they wanted Saturday to be a half-day instead of the full working day it was at present. They also wished to be excused work on Christmas Day, Good Friday and the Bank Holidays. Last of all, they wanted recognition of their right to be union members. But the farmers refused to yield.

By late June an estimated 800 men were on strike in and around the villages of Helions Bumpstead, Steeple Bumpstead, Birdbrook, Ridgewell, Ashdon and

Sturmer in Essex, and into Cambridgeshire at Weston Colville, Castle Camps and West Wickham, and in Suffolk at Withersfield. The men were buoyed by the knowledge that they were receiving between five and ten shillings weekly from a central strike fund. Added to this their position was strengthened as the local hay crop ripened and then became spoilt as it lay unattended in the fields. At the time the *Chronicle* reported that **'The farmers are suffering because the abstention of labour has allowed the land to get into a dreadful state. Root crops are choked with weeds, and the land generally will take a considerable time to recover from its foul condition.'** With the crucial corn harvest approaching farmers took desperate action, drafting in outside 'blackleg' men to labour alongside themselves and their families. In addition they requested and were given police protection in order to go about their work. By July it was a common, yet no less incredible sight, to see sizeable numbers of police, including some Metropolitan constables, patrolling lanes, standing sentry at farm gates and guarding men at work in the fields.

A SENSE OF PANIC

It was at this stage of the strike that trouble really began. At Ashdon in early July eight men were arrested and charged for trying to disrupt strike-breaking work on a local farm. The eight were fined between £1 and £2 each. All refused to pay and instead walked to Saffron Walden police station with a view to surrendering themselves. As the *Chronicle* reported, they were accompanied by **'a procession of some 200 strikers from Ashdon, Sturmer, Ridgewell, and other affected parishes, and by banner bearers. Flags were carried on hay-rakes and hedge-poles.'** After this incident bad-feeling escalated and a sense of panic seems to have spread, a situation not aided by the *Chronicle*'s claims that the strikers were now **'arming themselves with cudgels and sticks for riot'**. These fears were never realised, but nonetheless violence did occur. At Helions Bumpstead farmers were attacked as they attempted to rescue the hay crop. While at Steeple Bumpstead police were forced to close the Fox and Hounds public house as they anticipated a disturbance, only to find that this led to **'a lively scene in the street'** in which stones were thrown and shop windows broken. At Ashdon a group of strikers **'marched through the village shouting and singing loudly'**. They then **'began to stone the police, P.C. Gatey and P.C. Burton being hit. The police then drew their truncheons, and the strikers moved a distance off where they remained for an hour'**.

A wide range of causes now began to embrace the labourers. The powerful Dockers Union contributed to the strike fund, Labour MP George Lansbury addressed the strikers' meetings, as did the leading Suffragette, Sylvia

Strikers, their families and police pose for the camera at Ashdon. The strike was not always so peaceful

Source: Essex Countryside Magazine

LABOURERS' STRIKE

FARMERS FIRM.

POLICE DRAFTED INTO N.-W. ESSEX.

Pankhurst. In late July the Bishop of Chelmsford's attempts at conciliation led to a meeting of both sides at which the union agreed to drop its pay claim to fifteen shillings a week, but the farmers refused to raise their offer from fourteen and a half shillings. Just six pence now stood between the parties. Public sympathy started to tip the way of the strikers, a case aided when the eight men of Ashdon, fined for their part in disturbances, were imprisoned for their refusal to pay. The *Chronicle* echoed the public mood when it called on **'the farmers to concede something, so as to bring a wasteful struggle to a close in time for the gathering of the corn'**.

Then, on Saturday 1st August, came the most serious incident in this summer of struggle. That night, under the cover of darkness, arsonists struck at five hay stacks in the villages of Birdbrook and Steeple Bumpstead. **'The stacks were situated within half a mile of one another, and all were lighted simultaneously, between nine and ten o'clock. The night was very dark, the countryside was quickly illuminated.'**

The fires appeared to signal a new depth to the worsening relationships between farmers and labourers. Until that point disturbances had been limited to attempts at stopping work; now they had turned to the large-scale destruction of property. The outlook appeared bleak. Fields stood ready for harvest. If the strike continued they would be lost.

CALL TO PATRIOTISM

Yet within three days of the arson attacks the strike was suddenly over. Throughout the passing months of summer a bigger conflict had been stirring on the European mainland. On 4th August 1914 Britain declared war on Germany and the strike which had dominated the passions of people in north Essex was flooded by a greater cause. As the *Chronicle* pointed out, the call to **'the patriotism of the farmers and the labourers engaged in the struggle'** had proved too great to ignore. Some men returned to a week's work which remained six days long, but at least now gave them a newly agreed wage of fifteen shillings. Others joined the forces in readiness to fight.

Still, the importance of the 1914 strike should not be understated. It was not on the scale of the General Strike that was to follow in 1926 (see chapter six). Nor did it catch the national attention, as other labour disputes did both before and after it. However, the strike did show that there were chinks in the facade of the English countryside, a place that seemed to be a peaceful haven from the rush, the bustle, the turmoil of modern, urban Edwardian life. The strike had not simply been about poor pay. It was also a rebellion against the other trappings of rural poverty; the poor housing that many suffered, the

Harvest workers pause for the camera in Latchingdon

1914 THE ESSEX COUNTRYSIDE IN DISPUTE 17

A hard furrow: farm workers were and remain amongst the poorest paid in Essex

winter unemployment they shouldered, the lack of village amenities and the deference that was expected by local farmers and the gentry. Finally, the strike also stood as proof with which to undermine the popular stereotype (often still held) that agricultural labourers and their families were slow, dull-witted people, unable to help themselves out of their predicament.

That was the time when...

The *Essex County Chronicle* was advertising the new range of Kodak cameras at 30 shillings a piece, along with the message that **'Kodak will give you a complete picture of your summer holiday from the time you take your railway ticket until you get home again. A Kodak will give you an album of jolly snapshots that will keep the memory of your holiday always green.'**

Meanwhile other bargains could be had. Smart Brothers of Stratford were offering readers **'furniture of quality, dependability and artistic excellence'** such as a **'solid oak bedroom suite, wardrobe, dressing table, washstand with marble top, and two chairs'** for £8 8s.

Perhaps less of a bargain were the many advertisements carried by the paper which claimed to cure what were euphemistically called **'women's ailments'** or **'women's blockages'**. Of these 'Widow Welch's Female Pills' promised **'prompt and reliable action for ladies'** along with the reassurance that they had been **'awarded a certificate of merit at the Tasmanian Exhibition of 1891 - 1s. a box'**.

Even with war fast approaching there was no shortage of entertainment to be found. The new Parade Cinema at Brentwood was offering a programme which included **'the great picture - Anthony and Cleopatra'**, alongside slightly less known titles such as 'In the Lion's Cage', 'Wiffles Tricks the Detectives', 'Above and Below' and the intriguingly titled 'Life in a Fresh Water Aquarium'. Seats were priced at 3d, 6d and 1s in what was billed as **'The best ventilated hall in the county. Cool in the warmest evening.'**

As the Great War moved slowly to its end Essex faced yet another challenge. The war had claimed the lives of many of the county's young men, as well as maiming and traumatising countless others. Yet in October 1918, within weeks of the armistice, a further threat to life began to emerge. Unlike the bloody deaths met by those in the mud of foreign battlefields, this was a silent and bloodless threat which struck at home. But it was a remorseless killer nonetheless, for it was the sheer scale of the influenza epidemic of 1918 that made it such a dramatic event in the county's history...

1918 INFLUENZA EPIDEMIC: 'the sickness rages'

HEALTH, BOTH PERSONAL and public, was something that preoccupied the *Essex County Chronicle* and its readers in the early decades of the twentieth century. It is easy to understand why, at a time when a comprehensive National Health Service remained an unfulfilled ideal for social reformers, and when medical insurance remained patchy, especially amongst the poor. If illness did strike, calling a doctor in 1918 was often the last, expensive resort for families, rather than their first consideration. Little wonder then that the pages of the *Chronicle* featured so many advertisements for inexpensive pills, syrups, tinctures and balms covering a wide range of ailments such as indigestion, piles, sore throats, colds, gout, headaches, and so on. The claims made for these 'medicines' were often dramatic, although the actual results may well have been less startling. In addition to these many people still relied upon an armoury of home-remedies, folk-remedies and even superstitions to keep ill-health from their doors.

The general health of the county's people was better in 1918 than it had been in the mid nineteenth century and it continued to improve throughout the coming decades. People were now living longer. Nationally the average life expectancy in 1910 was 52 years for men and 55 for women. By 1938 it was 61 for men and 66 for women. Levels of infant mortality, the number of deaths per thousand children under the age of 1 year, tumbled from 142 in 1900 to 31 in 1950. Contemporary surveys also show that school children were growing taller and heavier, and were less likely to fall victim to childhood complaints such as rickets, whooping cough and scarlet fever, while the big killers such as tuberculosis, diphtheria and typhoid began to show signs of decline.

On the whole it was not the breakthroughs of medical science which were at the root of these improvements. Many, if not most, of the population lay outside the reach of regular formal health care and medicine. Instead we can thank a set of basic measures including the gradual provision of clean water, more housing with greater space and better sanitation, slowly rising living standards and better diets. Education was also a key, leading increasing numbers of people to the understanding that a few simple preventative

Nurses and convalescing soldiers pose during the 1914-18 war

measures could go a significant way towards ensuring healthiness. However, in the spring of 1918 there was an outbreak of a disease that neither medicine nor the basic improvements in health care could do much to repel. The disease was influenza.

There seems little agreement as to the origin of the 1918 virus. The Essex press quickly dubbed it the 'Spanish Flu', but there appears to have been no firm evidence for this name. However, its virulence could not be doubted as the strain spread not merely across countries but continents, claiming an estimated 50 million lives world-wide, in what one historian has called *'one of the severest holocausts of disease ever encountered'*. In Britain the epidemic, which was at its severest in late 1918 and which surfaced again early in 1919, killed around 150,000 men, women and children, and created one of the biggest public health crises of the twentieth century.

The first signs of the epidemic appeared in the Essex press during early October 1918. At Wimbish it was reported that Mr L. Drysdale of New House Farm had passed away aged 38 years after *'just a few hours illness, and the same day a maidservant in the house also died'*. This was a pattern that was to be repeated again and again over coming months as the virus struck whole households, sometimes killing several members.

By mid October concern was spreading fast as each of the new outbreaks was recorded. Southend was said to be suffering with *'several hundred cases of the disease, and a number of deaths have occurred. Nearly 3,000 children have been away from school ill. Also about 50 teachers are incapacitated.'* At Chelmsford, Ilford and Colchester, as well as at a host of villages, schools were shut. 200 children in Witham were reported to be *'ill at home'*, while in Romford it was said that 50 per cent of children were absent, either ill with the flu, or kept away by fearful parents.

THEORY AND PREVENTION

J.C. Thresh, the county's Medical Officer, believed the epidemic to be *'spreading along the lines of the railway - London to Southend, London to Epping, London to Waltham Cross, and along the main Colchester and Cambridge lines'*. Thresh went on to promote his theory that *'it is chiefly being spread by overcrowding in the railway carriages'*. As for prevention, he prescribed *'throat and nose disinfection'* with a *'solution of permanganate of potash'*, while also recommending that *'rooms used for meetings of children and adults should be sprayed with a 2 per cent solution of formalin'*. But for those unfortunate enough to be struck down there was little else to do but wait and see if the virus would pass. On this point Thresh was able to offer readers only the most meagre comfort and advice: *'The present form of influenza is rather more rapid in its attack than any previous one. Anyone feeling at all queer should keep quiet for 24 hours and take his temperature, and if it goes up he should go to bed at once. In some cases, however, there is not even the time to wait for that test, and bed and nursing are immediately necessary.'*

The *Chronicle* believed it to be the young, especially those in their teens, twenties and thirties who were most susceptible, and the reports of deaths from around the county do seem to lend this some support. It was certainly amongst this group that many of the most tragic tales emerged. For example, at Saffron Walden four died in a single cottage household including the mother, her two daughters and an infant grandchild, leaving only a single survivor. Or at Epping, where, as the parents of a teenage victim were burying her, influenza also took the life of their remaining daughter. At the Essex Record Office there still exists a letter from a mother to her daughter who is serving as a nurse in a French field hospital. The letter dated the 5th November 1918 tells of the death of the nurse's cousin, a young woman of nineteen. It describes the slow and painful end to the young woman's life and how they *'can never forget the last few hours. It was so awful watching her die - she had morphine but there were terrible choking struggles'*, and how they *'could only pray to God to let her die...Those few days ending with this trauma have been a ghastly strain.'*

Chelmsford General Hospital c.1918

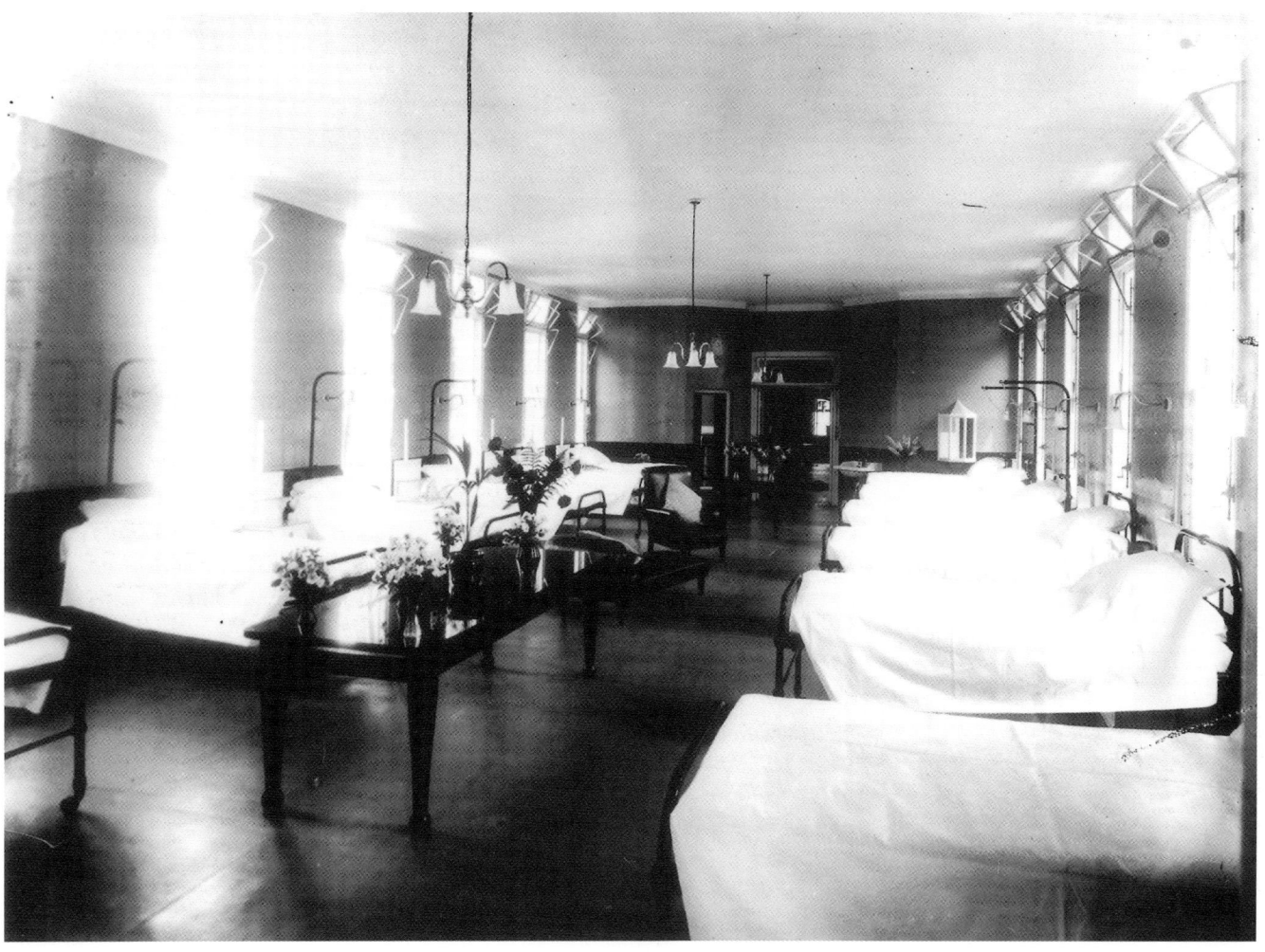

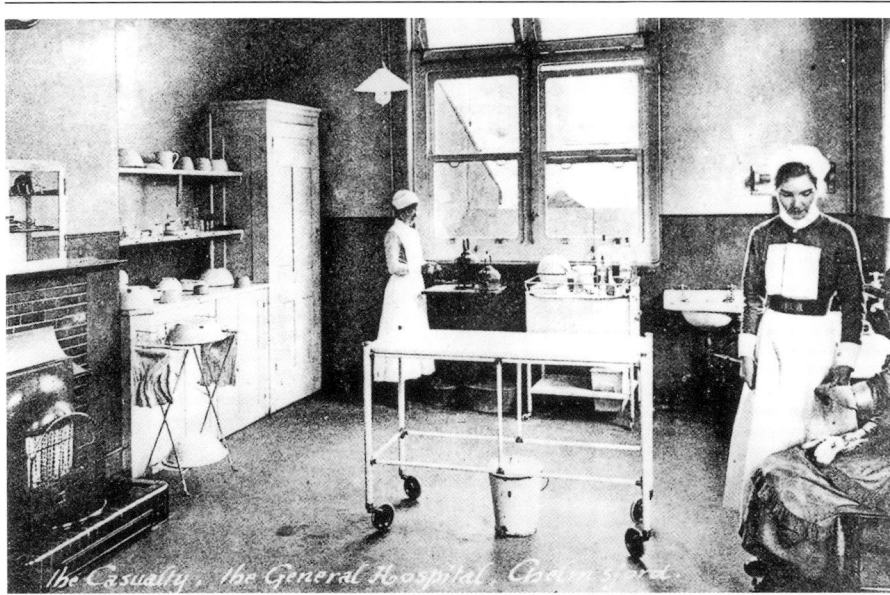

Casualty as it was in Chelmsford General Hospital c.1920

For many the relief felt at the news of the armistice signed on the 11th November must have been tinged with anxiety that the flu might yet strike them. Around this time the *Chronicle* carried reports of joyous celebrations around the county at the war's end, but alongside these came more solemn accounts of the progress of the epidemic. The newspaper's conclusion that ***'The scourge of influenza is still rampant, each day bringing additional victims'*** was grim but accurate. At Ilford, such was the scale of casualties that military help was being used ***'for the digging of graves'***. At Colchester the police force was said to be seriously under strength on account of the numbers of officers being ill at home, while at Bishop's Stortford it was said that ***'about half the population is ill'***. But it was the old metropolitan Essex boroughs with their high and densely packed populations that seem to have suffered worst of all. Here the *Chronicle* detailed some frightening figures, with the first week of November alone bringing ***'deaths from influenza which numbered 67 at East Ham, 62 at Leyton, 87 at Walthamstow, 100 in West Ham'***.

HEALTH OF THE NATION

Gradually the epidemic relented. By December there were fewer reported deaths, and although influenza did return to the county in February and March 1919 its reappearance did not compare in scale or virulence. However, the impact of the epidemic stayed with people for years to come. The *Chronicle* was left fearing for the long term health and fitness of the British nation. As it observed ***'Darwin taught us that the struggle for existence led to the survival of the fittest, but what is happening now reverses the process, for the influenza has a selective tendency for the strongest, the fittest, the most promising young adults.'*** Furthermore it saw a specific problem in that ***'young women seem to have withstood the epidemic better than young men, but thousands of them will go single for want of husbands...Altogether the outlook is not bright.'*** Seeing what it thought was a threat to the blood stock of the nation, the *Chronicle* put forward its own solutions: ***'every assistance should be given to those of our soldiers and sailors who are left to us to marry at once. Economic barriers should be removed; inducement should be held out.'*** Perhaps more surprisingly, the paper added, ***'the unmarried mother must be helped and protected. It is a matter of national urgency.'***

Despite these concerns the lasting memory of the influenza epidemic for most people was a personal one. For many families who had lived through the

22 HEADLINE HISTORY

SPANISH "FLU" AND GAS.
Wonderful Cures by the Old Remedy—
Veno's Lightning Cough Cure.

L/Corporal A. J. Turner, of the 4th Essex Regiment, writes:—"I was in hospital, and lying opposite me was a sergeant in the R.F.A., who had been badly gassed. It was awful to hear him coughing night and day. Knowing Veno's, I told him of it, and from the first dose all the fellows in the ward noticed a decrease in his coughing. In six weeks that same man proceeded to a convalescent hospital in my company. Two men and myself affected with Spanish "Flu" found instantaneous relief in Veno's."

Veno's Lightning Cough Cure is the world's supreme remedy for Coughs and Colds, Lung Troubles, Asthma, Bronchitis, Nasal Catarrh, Hoarseness, Difficult Breathing, and Influenza. Specially recommended for Whooping Cough and Bronchial Troubles
11½d., 1~ 3d
Sto~

Advertisers were not afraid to use the 'flu to increase sales offering the public 'relief' and 'cures'

 1918

Our earliest CD extract takes us back to the last days of the First World War. John Hewitt (born 1904) was one of the survivors of a virus that was to take the lives of many Essex people during 1918 and 1919. His experiences contrast with those of Albert King (born 1902), for whom influenza seems to have offered opportunity in a job market which was beginning to be flooded by the return of demobbed soldiers.
TO LISTEN SELECT CD TRACK 1

four long years of the war, with its fear that at any moment a son, husband or father might be taken from them, the flu epidemic had proved to be a bitter and unexpected final twist. Take, for example, the story of Private H. Mansfield of the 17th Lancers, who returned from the Western Front to his Essex village of Newport in February of 1919. We can only guess at his family's relief at their son having survived the German shells and bullets. But then we can only wonder how quickly this joy turned to grief, as within hours of his homecoming the young soldier *'fell a victim of influenza and pneumonia'*, and at the family's horror as he was followed swiftly by his mother and sister. Within a week all three were dead.

That was the time when...

The plans for reconstruction after the war were well under way. In February 1919 Essex County Council announced a spending programme totalling £3 million which was to provide new roads, railways and houses in the county.

The *Chronicle* also reported on other plans, this time on a proposed channel tunnel link. The tunnel had first been started over a hundred years before but had been aborted. Now it was said that *'At last it seems as if the project of a tunnel from Dover to Calais will be realised'*. Confidence certainly seems to have been high as it was said *'Supporters are already talking of direct train communication between London and Calcutta'*.

Elsewhere, the newspaper's classified advertisements show that advertisers were not slow to see a business situation from even the bleakest of news. Several advertisements appear offering either guard against or else cure for influenza. *'Don't Run Risks! NOSTROLINE nasal specific will protect you against Influenza, Nasal Catarrh, Head Colds, and other infectious disorders'*, promised one. *'It destroys the germs and soothes nose and throat. Delays are dangerous. Get it now. Of leading chemists everywhere - 1s 3d.'*

Chelmsford, World War One

In May 1926 Essex was caught up in twentieth century Britain's most dramatic episode of industrial unrest. While the Trade Union movement and the Government were locked in struggle for nine days, county and country were brought to a standstill as trains, buses and trams ceased to run, the post was stopped and fears of food and fuel shortages spread...

1926 THE GENERAL STRIKE: 'no time for compromise'

IN THE EARLY spring of 1926 thoughts of general industrial strife affecting the county must have seemed remote. It was true that Britain was witnessing industrial unrest, but this was centred on the coal fields of the north where miners were attempting to fight wage cuts and increased hours. The *Essex Chronicle* was certainly unaware of the dramatic events that were beginning to unfold about it. Looking back now, its short reports on the coal dispute appear complacent. But at the time it must all have seemed a long way away from Essex.

However, by Monday 3rd May this distant dispute had come to mean much more, for in the space of three days national action had been called for by the Trades Union Congress (TUC) and Essex, alongside all other areas of the country, was suddenly in the midst of the General Strike.

The General Strike might have been triggered by the coal miners' dispute, but its roots lay much deeper. Trade Union strength across the country and throughout different industries had been growing since the late nineteenth century. Union membership which had stood at just over 1.5 million in the early 1890s had swollen to over 5 million by 1926. Trade Union power had also grown. Unions were now widely recognised by employers and had succeeded in pushing up wage levels and in reducing the working week, while in the First World War they had been invited to join employers and government in negotiations and strategic economic planning. However, by 1926 the economy was beginning to stall and enter a period of extreme depression. Alongside growing numbers joining the dole queues came pressure from employers to reduce wages and increase the working week. The General Strike was seen as a final opportunity by unions to halt these trends.

THE ESSEX SCENE

Essex had no large scale heavily unionised industry such as coal or steel. The impact of the strike was therefore indirect, but nonetheless startling. Some factory workforces did come out. At the Crittall works at Braintree a visiting reporter for the *Essex Chronicle* **'found them empty of workmen. A crowd of men gathered outside the works had made their headquarters at the Labour Club opposite.'** Despite the seriousness of the dispute the reporter seemed relieved that **'Everything was peaceful and friendly.'** Elsewhere a portion of

---

THE FOURTH DAY OF THE GREAT STRIKE.

LATEST NEWS.

SPECIAL REPORTS UP TO THIS MORNING.

PRIME MINISTER'S MESSAGE

ADVENTURES ON THE ROAD

SENTENCE ON MR. SAKLATVALA

Hit by paper shortages and transport problems, the Essex Chronicle still carried news of the strike to its readers

the Marconi workforce had struck at Chelmsford, while the Ind Coope brewery at Romford was closed as men picketed its gates.

But it was the railwaymen who created most disruption. In Essex, as elsewhere, support for the strike was solid upon the railways. Their influence was dramatic, literally bringing Essex to a standstill at a time when rail remained the chief form of long distance travel for freight and person. By the third day of the strike the London and North-Eastern Railway running out of London Liverpool Street into Essex had been reduced to a *'skeleton service'*. At Chelmsford it was reported that *'all the employees are out'*. Commuting was made impossible. On Wednesday 5th May only two trains ran on the line between London and Norwich. *'They conveyed chiefly parcels and mail, but there were a few passengers, one of whom alighted at Chelmsford.'*

Rail problems ensured that the county's roads were now clogged with extra traffic. It was reported that travelling in and out of London from the county was *'worse than on Derby day. Yesterday it took vehicles two and a half hours to get from Romford to Bow.'* Police advised drivers to *'avoid starting for home at rush hours and make use of side roads and alternative routes to the main roads'*. Drivers were also asked to help those who usually relied on the now defunct public transport system by displaying a notice in their cars saying *'If you want a lift, please signal'*.

UNCERTAINTY AND PANIC

The General Strike crumbled after only nine days, but during this time the uncertainty as to how long it would last began to create panic. Perhaps unwittingly, the *Essex Chronicle* contributed to these fears. Under the headline of *'The Appeal to Reason'*, the paper described the General Strike as a crisis greater than when the Spanish Armada or Napoleon's troops threatened Britain's shores, and greater still than when British troops faced Germany in the trenches of northern France.

Some shortages began to be reported and others feared. Food and fuel were most at threat as people began to buy-up and hoard essential supplies. On 7th May the paper warned that *'The public should assist in maintaining a fair distribution of supplies by refraining from buying more than their usual quantities of foodstuffs and coal'*. Everywhere price increases on meat, milk and bread were reported. At Brentwood coal was rationed, while the Urban District Council made an attempt to reassure local people with the statement that it was *'confident'* of being able to cope with whatever was to come. But in Braintree the mood seems to have been less buoyant. Here the Rural District Council's meeting was begun with councillors joining in a minute's silent prayer for the ending of the strike and the survival of the town.

The survival of Braintree and the rest of the county was due partly to the emergency measures introduced by national and local government. Throughout Essex control centres were staffed and invested with *'emergency powers'* to safeguard vital supplies and to maintain some order. The headquarters for the Essex operations were in Colchester, stationed at the *'Standard Ironworks, telephone Colchester 82'*. Other offices existed at Chelmsford, Harwich, Clacton, Maldon, Brentwood, Grays, Southend, Romford, Braintree, Epping and Saffron Walden. All were assisted in their task by the Essex Constabulary who were strengthened by some hastily enrolled Special Constables.

Generally the strike in Essex was calm and ordered, but violence did sometimes occur. At Tilbury, for example, a train manned by police was attacked by a *'hostile crowd of about 500 people, who commenced to throw stones. Four carriage windows were broken.'* The signal wires were cut by the crowd, a policeman injured and three men arrested. Two of the arrested were imprisoned with hard labour for fourteen days, the third was fined £3. At

Essex Chronicle 7th May 1926

The General Strike saw some workers at Marconi's in Chelmsford down tools. Here the men of the firm's carpentry shop are photographed c.1930

Stanford-le-Hope a convoy of ten motor lorries, again under police escort, transporting oil between Ilford and Thames Haven, met a crowd of 300 men. The crowd were reported to have shouted that they wished revenge on special constables who had beaten and abused them. A fight ensued and here again one policeman was injured.

The muscle of policemen was not the only means by which order was kept and a semblance of normality preserved. Government was also quick to use the media to spread its message of calm and its appeal to unity. The Conservative Government, under Prime Minister Stanley Baldwin, launched its own national newspaper the *British Gazette* under the editorship of Winston Churchill. Alongside this the BBC carried regular reports and appeals from Government into the homes of many through the new medium of wireless radio. The *Essex Chronicle* too played its part as throughout it adopted a solidly anti-strike stance. On 7th May it even carried an address to the people of Essex from Prime Minister Baldwin which appealed to the *'good citizens'* of the county to *'Stand behind the Government, who are doing their part. The laws of England are the people's birthright. The laws are in your keeping. You have made Parliament their guardian. The General Strike is a challenge to Parliament, and is the road to anarchy and ruin.'*

POWER IN THE UNION

On Wednesday 12th May the *Essex Chronicle* announced the end of the General Strike by posting notices in the windows of its main offices in Chelmsford. The paper later reported that *'The news spread like wildfire. While everybody was delighted and relieved, there were no undue signs of excitement. Newspapers were bought eagerly.'* Trade Union leaders had called off the dispute. Slowly life resumed its normal patterns, food and fuel supplies were restored, public transport ran once more, the post was delivered and people got back to work. However, the General Strike had shown the people of Essex the potential power of trade union action. The events of May 1926 also foreshadowed the desperate industrial problems that were to come with the depression of the late 1920s and early 1930s.

That was the time when...

The Personal column of the *Chronicle* was already acting as a place for 'lonely hearts'. For example, one advertisement read *'Bachelor, 32, good position, invites correspondence from single lady, 24-30, refined, pianist.'*

Alongside came advertisements for the publications of the birth control reformer Dr Marie Stopes: *'A Letter to Working Mothers, 3d; Wise Parenthood, 3s 6d; Married Love 6s'*... While other advertisements promised freedom through better health: *'Constipation: civilisation's curse - Beecham's Pills stimulate bowels...'*

Elsewhere, new motor cars were on sale, models such as the Morris Cowley, available for £162, or Fiats for £295 and Renaults £219.

It was the time of year when men might be thinking of a new spring suit. Perhaps *'A particularly smart whipcord, in the new shade of Bronze Brown'* in the shops priced at just 45s.

House buyers were being tempted to move to the New Town Estate in Braintree where £425 could purchase a home with *'Four bedrooms, front and back parlour, kitchen, bathroom, pantry and outbuildings, all freehold; standing in their own ground'*.

Home entertainment was centred around the BBC, which promised an evening's listening to *'Schumann: Interpreted by Isobel Gray; the Novelty Minstrels: entirely composed of coloured artists; Time Signal from Greenwich and News Bulletin; Percy Edgar, in Recitals Grave and Gay; and Dance Music: The Savoy Orpheans and Savoy Tango Bands, relayed from the Savoy Hotel'*.

In 1926 women's fashion and beauty still involved subjugation to the corset

---

1926

As a railway worker Jack Ashton (born 1902) belonged to one of the most highly unionised and militant occupations in Essex. In May 1926 Jack and other railwaymen joined the General Strike and briefly, but dramatically, brought the county to a standstill

TO LISTEN SELECT CD TRACK 2

Crime, including assaults, drunkenness, car-theft, burglary, mugging, might all appear to be an unfortunate part of modern life, a distressing development of more recent times. Yet throughout the late nineteenth and early twentieth centuries all these crimes and more besides were reported in the Essex Chronicle with a regularity that suggests that they have been with us longer than we like to think. Yet in 1927 a crime took place that shocked and outraged people then as it would do today. For on one foggy early September morning a policeman was cycling along the deserted lanes of his village beat. Within minutes he had been shot, killed by four well-aimed bullets to his head...

1927 THE MURDER OF P.C. GUTTERIDGE: 'men without hope'

DURING THE NIGHT of 30 May 1928 Frederick Browne wrote his last letter. The next day he was to be executed with his accomplice, William Kennedy, for the murder of P.C. William George Gutteridge. The letter neither asked for mercy nor for pardon, but spoke scornfully of having **'little desire to live one hour longer in such an unjust world'**, and of a final hope that one day **'the true facts leak out'** in what had been one of the most dramatic murder cases ever to have occurred in Essex.

More than seventy years on, the case shows few signs of yielding any of the **'true facts'** which would disprove the guilty verdicts placed on either Browne or Kennedy. Reading the lengthy trial reports in the *Essex Chronicle*, the murder appears as a straightforward case. Gutteridge had been in the wrong place at the wrong time, when on the early morning of 27th September 1927 he was patrolling his rural beat at Stapleford Abbots in the west of Essex. It was around 3.30am when he met up with Browne and Kennedy as they drove along the quiet lanes. Why Gutteridge decided to stop the men never became clear. Perhaps they were speeding, for at the trial people living close to the scene spoke of being woken in their beds by a motor car travelling recklessly fast. Even more baffling was why Browne and Kennedy consented to stop. The *Essex Chronicle* later described both as **'well-known car-bandits'**. Indeed, the car they were now travelling in had been stolen earlier that night from a doctor's garage in Billericay. But now, faced with a rural policeman, who stood before them without a radio, whose only form of transport was his standard issue police bicycle, and who was armed only with a truncheon and a whistle, the two men when signalled to do so drew up in their car. From that moment the fate of all three was sealed.

Gutteridge was found a couple of hours later by a van driver on his way to the first delivery of his day. The policeman was dead, pools of blood lay under him and across the road. **'A lead pencil was grasped in the constable's right hand, and his notebook was lying open by his side. His helmet lay a few feet**

THE MURDERED CONSTABLE
A RECENT PHOTOGRAPH OF P.C. W. G. GUTTERIDGE,
Reproduced by the courtesy of the "Daily Mail."

Essex Chronicle 30th September 1927

ESSEX POLICEMAN MURDERED

FOUND SHOT AT STAPLEFORD ABBOTS

GRIM EARLY MORNING DISCOVERY

STARTLING DEVELOPMENTS

One of the most remarkable crimes of recent years, claiming as its victim a popular Essex policeman, murdered in the actual performance of his duty, sent a wave of consternation over the county on ~~~~~~ While the countryside was still enshrouded in ~ Police-con~~~~~ ~~~~ William Gutter~~

away. His whistle was out of his pocket, and his cape was thrown over his shoulders.' Gutteridge had been shot four times, apparently while trying to record details about the men and their vehicle. As gruesome as this scene was, it was made more so by the discovery that two of the shots had been aimed through the eyes of the constable and that *'The shots through the eyes had been fired with the revolver held almost up against his face...the skin was blackened and burned'*.

However, the murder of P.C. Gutteridge, its subsequent investigation, the trial and the executions of Browne and Kennedy tell much more than a simple, sad story of a needless loss of life. Take, for example, the manner in which Browne and Kennedy were apprehended and then found guilty. In part the case against them lay in a confession from Kennedy in which he admitted to being present at the murder, but in which he also claimed it had been Browne who had fired the gun. But this alone was not enough to convict Browne, who always denied being at the scene, an alibi his wife's testimony to the court supported. More evidence was needed, but as the *Chronicle* reported, the investigation was faced with a set of *'baffling circumstances...Not a single clue of value, and no apparent motive'*. But the newspaper and perhaps the murderers had not bargained for the new developments that were beginning to aid police work in the 1920s.

THE CASE BUILDS
Within hours of the murder the Essex force called in the Metropolitan Police to assist in the investigation. At the time, detectives from the London force represented the cutting-edge of police work, and a crime which had appeared to offer so little was soon beginning to yield them clues.

The stolen car was quickly found in south London, and as the *Chronicle* reported, *'Finger print experts from Scotland Yard were called to examine the abandoned car. They brought their special finger print blowing apparatus, and worked on the car for some hours.'* What they found was a number of prints, some belonging to Gutteridge, some to the car's owner Dr Lovell, but also some that were unknown to the police. When Browne and Kennedy were arrested in January 1928 for the theft of a further car, their fingerprints were found to match these. The case against them was beginning to build.

However, fingerprinting had been available to the police from the first years of the twentieth century. And fingerprints offered only circumstantial evidence that either man had participated in the murder. But the crime scene gave officers more than mere fingerprints. Two of the bullets which had killed the constable were recovered from the murder scene, while a spent cartridge was also found in the stolen car. It was evidence from these that satisfied both police, and eventually the jury, of Browne and Kennedy's guilt. The Gutteridge murder was to be one of the first in which the emerging forensic science of ballistics was to play a crucial part. With the help of experts at Woolwich arsenal, police were able to match not only the bullets with the cartridge, but also the bullets with a revolver found in Browne's possession on the day of his arrest. It had been a recent scientific discovery that each gun left its own individual imprint on the rounds fired from it. Painstaking microscopic investigation of the two bullets showed that they held a unique pattern which matched that of Browne's revolver. It was this that clinched the case against the men.

PUBLIC REACTION

Today it is a frequently heard complaint that violence has reached unprecedented levels, that we live in a society of dwindling standards and an absence of respect. The treatment of our police is often used as a starting point for these complaints. It is said that the police now elicit less respect, less reverence, and face more antagonism in conducting their duties than they once did. The killing of P.C. Gutteridge suggests that we might need to place this view of the past into a fuller context. As the *Essex Chronicle* highlighted, Gutteridge's death was the third case in living memory of an Essex policeman being murdered while on duty. Of the others, one had been shot and the other had had his throat cut. But it was the Bishop of Romford, presiding at Gutteridge's funeral, who thought that he detected something more in the policeman's death, something which threatened the very fabric of Essex life itself. He told the packed congregation:

'We would like to think such a deed would have been more likely among the wilder tribes who live in other parts of the world. They [the murderers] must be desperadoes - men without hope. It seems so un-English; yet I am afraid it is typical of the spirit that is beginning to find some development among us - a spirit that is not only regardless of property, which is a small matter, but which thinks nothing of the value of human life, or the affection of human life which binds a man to those he loves more than life itself.'

The Gutteridge murder did shock Essex, at first holding its people in a state of revulsion at the killing, and then in macabre intrigue as the case moved on towards its finale with the executions of Browne and Kennedy. For a newspaper like the *Chronicle*, the violent death of a police officer was big news and represented an ideal way in which to grip existing readers and tempt in others. As a consequence its coverage was extensive and quickly became a heady, if not always accurate, mix which sought to make much of the violent detail. For example, early reports from the paper claimed that Gutteridge had *'actually jumped on the running boards [of the car], and was grappling with the driver when the shots were fired.'* Yet later reports from the trial carried a story of much less dramatic events. Instead it seems Gutteridge had been shot as he bent down to record the car's number plate. There had been no grappling and no last dramatic struggle.

Elsewhere the *Chronicle* aimed directly at its readers' hearts, playing up the murder's tragic content. Alongside harrowing detail of the murder scene were descriptions of Gutteridge's widow, their two young children and above all the domestic haven that the murder had now destroyed. *'At the time of the tragedy'*, explained the paper, *'P.C. Gutteridge was on the way to his home, where breakfast and his wife were awaiting him in the small ivy-covered cottage, standing in a delightful little garden. Instead of her husband returning, Mrs Gutteridge answered a knock on the door by a sorrowing fellow constable, who broke the sad news as gently as he could. It was a terrible moment.'* The funeral, held at Warley, was said to have been attended by *'200 of the dead man's colleagues'* who marched through crowds *'rows deep'* along streets that were silent except for *'the steady tramp of the passing policemen, and the half-smothered sobs of onlookers'*. The detail extended to Mrs Gutteridge who was said to be *'truly a pathetic figure'* as she had to be *'almost carried to her seat. Her eyes closed, her drawn face ashen, and her mouth was set as in grief which is beyond tears.'*

The murdered constable's children, Muriel, aged 12 and William, aged 4

FUND FOR FAMILY

After the funeral the *Essex Chronicle* quickly advertised a special fund for Gutteridge's widow. Its aim was to raise £100 to add to her modest police pension. After all it was difficult to think of a more deserving case. But public attention and sympathy proved fickle. Less than two months after the murder, in a small back-page article, the *Chronicle* announced that the fund was to be closed. It had raised just £60. Its organisers were left reflecting that they were *'sorry to see subscriptions coming in so slowly'*.

From here on little mention is made of Mrs Gutteridge and the struggle she faced in coping with a young family without her husband and his wage. Public attention and that of the *Chronicle* turned instead to his murderers; it was they who now offered the drama. Throughout their arrests, committals and trials the newspaper carried details of them, their lives, their wives and families, their protestations of innocence and even details about both men's attempts at suicide while in custody. But it was their executions that offered most dramatic detail and generated most excitement. Both men were hung at 9am on 31st May 1928, Browne at Pentonville prison and Kennedy at Wandsworth prison. As the hour approached large crowds gathered outside each venue. Although executions were no longer public affairs, some people were not to be denied a view. Outside Pentonville *'people got on to crates, boxes and walls. Every window of the houses overlooking the prison seemed to be occupied. As the prison clock struck 9am men raised their hats.'*

EXECUTION

In its reports the *Chronicle* was even able to give details of the men's last hours. Browne was said to have *'spent a final quiet evening in the cell. He did not speak when awakened at 8am, but had a fairly good breakfast, and sat awaiting the executioner'* whom he greeted with a polite *'Good morning'*. Kennedy by contrast had *'risen at 6am after a night spent in writing and reading. Until late at night he was still hopeful of a reprieve.'* Outside, *'a short distance from the prison'*, a *'taxicab drove up and stopped in the road.'* In it sat Kennedy's wife. The couple had only been married for six months. *'Dressed in deep mourning, her face hidden by a thick veil. She sat in the cab and watched the clock...As it struck nine, Mrs Kennedy broke down, and falling forward in the cab, burst into loud sobs and cries. The taxi drove away.'* An episode which had left three women widowed and three children without fathers had finally come to an end.

The accepted vision of the depression of the late 1920s and 1930s is one of northern industrial towns with their human chains of workless men queuing outside 'dole' offices, closed factory and mine gates, bleak, back-to-back housing and the Jarrow marchers. But Essex too, felt the cold grip of an economic slump. In the first week of 1930 the Chronicle greeted the New Year with a town-by-town survey reporting on the economic health of the county. The reports represent a fascinating testimony, not only to the extent of the depression, but to the morale of the county's people as they faced the most serious economic downturn of the century...

1930 THE DEPRESSION: 'the outlook is one of uncertainty'

THERE HAD BEEN economic slumps before. Many people in 1930 would have been able to remember the downturns of 1903-5 and 1908-10. The 1920s had also proved a bumpy economic ride in Britain, with the immediate post-war boom giving way to a downturn, before a degree of recovery in the middle of the decade. However, the Wall Street Crash of 1929 precipitated a recession whose severity was unimaginable and which was not going to be confined to North America. The growth in world trade, the improvements in inter-continental communications and commerce that were such a feature of the modern world now proved a double-edged sword. Like the influenza virus which had struck twelve years before, the collapse in business confidence proved highly contagious, spreading from country to country with dramatic effect. No economy was to be immune as nations and continents were plunged into depression.

In Britain the slump in world trade hit the industries that had once acted as cornerstones of the Victorian economy. Coal, shipbuilding, cotton, iron and steel production were hit worst of all. Their geographical concentration in parts of the midlands and the north of England, south Wales and in Scotland created pockets which contained bewildering levels of deprivation. By 1932 unemployment levels reached 41% amongst coal miners, 31% amongst cotton workers, 49% amongst iron and steel workers, and 60% in the shipyards.

Essex, as with much of the south and east of England, witnessed nothing on this scale. The depression had exposed the longer term problems of the British economy which was over-reliant upon the old, 'heavy' industries. However, no region could dodge the effects of the depression entirely. By 1931 British exports to the rest of the world stood at just half the level that they had been at the outbreak of World War One in 1914. Essex, even with its growing number of new and light industries, saw its factories' order books emptying. Unemployment, which had been at just 6% in 1929, quickly grew to 14% by 1932. Besides, one 'old' Essex industry still stood at the centre of many local economies, and it was experiencing its most bleak period since the 1880s. This was agriculture which, as we shall see, suffered severely during this time.

GLOOM, PERPLEXITY AND OPTIMISM

At least the local press seemed to be doing reasonably well. The *Essex Chronicle* could boast in 1930 that it had expanded to *'ten pages'* with its cost remaining at just one penny. Perhaps its readers could not afford a price rise, for on the inside pages of that year's first edition the *Chronicle* had surveyed every town in the county, checking on how each was withstanding the depression. The responses show a mixture of gloom, perplexity and optimism.

At Harwich the mayor, Mr Bernard, reported with sorrow that *'There are no signs that the town will take a sudden leap to greater prosperity'*. Although looking further ahead he was able to see hope on two fronts. At Dovercourt Bay he was expectant that *'with its natural beauties [it would] become more widely known, and increase in popularity with holiday makers'*. While for the town he foresaw great opportunities through its proximity to the European mainland, confidently predicting that *'Owing to its geographical position Harwich will, I believe, become an important air port'*.

Braintree too suffered in the present, but looked forward to a better future. Here it was admitted that *'The outlook for 1930 is the most serious known since the reconstruction after the war'*. Its report carried a baffled tone, bewildered at the way in which Braintree's manufacturing had been affected and complaining about the injustice of it all: *'so long as the products of Braintree - its metal windows, heavy motor castings and accessories, artificial silks - are of utilitarian value, they must command the markets of the world.'* It ends with what reads like a plea as much as a confident expectation regarding the future: *'Eventually Braintree goods will come into their own again, even now they encircle the globe. All trade and development at Braintree depends upon the prosperity of its manufactures'*.

Elsewhere, towns simply recorded a desire for better times. *'Colchester hopes that its unemployed will be considerably reduced'* was that town's

Essex farmers in discussion at the County Show of 1925

message for the coming year. At Maldon, where 300 men were out of work and on the books of the town's Employment Office, a succinct report simply read: *'The town generally has passed through a trying time.'* While in Walthamstow it was said that *'The outlook is one of uncertainty. Considerable anxiety is expressed in many quarters.'*

The depression did not settle evenly across towns and villages. Some communities escaped lightly. From the town-by-town reports of early 1930 Southend's reads like an oasis of calm and prosperity amongst the general suffering. Its self-proclaimed position as *'the shopping and amusement centre of South-east Essex'* was being bolstered by improvements made to its pier and by the provision of 200 trains which now travelled daily between the town and London. With this encouragement behind it, it was said that *'The town enjoyed a good season in 1929, and is looking forward to an even better one in 1930'.*

Chelmsford too, seemed to be aloof to the problems occurring elsewhere: *'Chelmsford is to be congratulated on its good fortune during the last year as, compared with the majority of other towns in the country, there has been little unemployment. It is in the fortunate position of having the majority of its industrial undertakings producing goods which are at present in great demand.'*

However, we might need to treat these claims with a degree of scepticism. For the reports in the *Chronicle* also highlight the attempts by some towns to 'talk up' their economic plights. Appearing optimistic, denying the existence of problems with failing manufacture and unemployment, represented a way in which to attract people, money and manufacture to an ailing community. Witham's statement, for example, reads less like a report on its economic health than as an advertisement for the town's self-proclaimed attractions:

'This town, situated in delightful surroundings, looks forward to the coming year as one in which prosperity may be on the increase. Admirably situated on the main thoroughfare and railway access of London and the port of Harwich, its prospects of development are bright, both as a residential and manufacturing centre.'

THE RURAL SCENE

However, it was in the Essex countryside that the economic slump hit hardest. Because so much of the imagery of the depression years is urban, it is easy to forget that the rural regions of Britain were also enduring hard times. But the world depression also meant tumbling agricultural market prices, as demand went into decline. The familiar 1930s picture of redundant factory machines and men lolling on street corners without work had their direct comparisons in villages. The depression struck at the markets in grain and arable farming with particular severity. Essex had long specialised in this very type of production and it was to suffer as a consequence. Essex grain, so long a source of pride and wealth, was now a burden. Each week the *Chronicle* carried reports on prices from around the county's markets. They paint a sombre picture. A typical report from early February 1930 reads: *'Braintree - wheat dull; Colchester - no real demand; Chelmsford - the complete market was in a depressed state, English grain being difficult to dispose of. Market described by buyers as a "chamber of horrors"'.*

Some farmers simply could not survive the crash. From the late 1920s onwards, the *Essex Chronicle* shows regular farm sales in its advertising columns, a sign that for some the battle had proved too much. However, most struggled on, but only at a price. Lifestyles were curbed, hunting, fishing and tennis parties reduced in number. Land was pulled from production, fields put down to grass, parts of farms left derelict and vital work went undone. To the

---

THE CRISIS IN AGRICULTURE

An advertisement appears on Page Six of THE ESSEX CHRONICLE to-day announcing a great demonstration for to-morrow, Saturday, March 1st, at 2.30 p.m., to be held on Parker's Piece, Cambridge, to demand immediate action by the Government to deal with the serious crisis in agriculture. Mr. E. G. Pretyman will be in the chair, and the chief speakers at the meeting, besides Mr. Pretyman himself, will be Captain Morris (President of the National Farmers' Union) and Mr. George Dallas, M.P. Cheap railway fares will be available at all stations to persons attending the demonstration. As THE ESSEX CHRONICLE holds the view that, not this Labour Government only, but any English Government, can render substantial aid to the farmer—especially the arable farmer—without indulging in any contentious policy and without affecting the living in other than t̶
we hope this meetin̶
Of the serious ̶
far at le̶
there c̶

Essex Chronicle 28th February 1930

urban person, exploring with hiking boots, a touring cycle or a motor car, the beauty of the Essex countryside at this time must have been breathtaking, with its over-grown hedges, abundant wildlife and wild flowers amongst crops. It seemed to represent a heady mix of rich colours, sounds and smells. But for the farm worker and his family, the same scene was one which spelled low wages, short-time in winter and even unemployment. To add to this, the agricultural labourer remained, until 1936, one of the few remaining occupations not to be covered by National Insurance and the 'dole' money that it provided. For some of the rural poor the only option which remained was the dreaded and distrusted system of 'parish relief', or Public Assistance as it was now called.

Throughout this crisis in the Essex countryside, the *Chronicle* presented a series of ready-made solutions, many sent in by their readers. It also reported odd sparks of militancy, such as an open-air demonstration in Cambridge in March 1930 which saw 10,000 farmers and their workers gather to hear a demand for *'immediate action by the Government to deal with the critical position of ploughland agriculture'*. But for most, the only answer seems to have been to sit tight and wait for good times to come again. As the Essex Farmers Union leader admitted with an air of resignation: *'We are passing through bad times, in fact I have never known worse, and when things are as bad as that, it is more than ever necessary that we should keep calm and level-headed'*.

However, the good times remained some way off. Only with the rising prices, Government assistance and a decline in imported food brought about by the coming of war in 1939 did Essex farming bloom once more. In the meantime, the state of its countryside was perfectly captured by the alternative 'harvest hymn' sent in by one farming reader in January 1930:

> 'We never plough nor scatter
> The good seed on the land;
> Because it does not matter,
> With German corn on hand.
> All the food around us
> Is sent from foreign parts;
> With ruined farms around us,
> And farmer's broken hearts.'

That was the time when...

While the prospects of the county for 1930 were being assessed, other stories featured in the January editions of the *Essex Chronicle*. Some bear a remarkable similarity with those of today.

Car crime seems to have been rife and a growing occupation, while single parent families were seen as part of the problem. Under the headline *'Joy Riders Surprise'* the newspaper reported the case of *'two very silly young men from Chelmsford, both in work, but unfortunately without fathers living, who went for "joy rides" in motor cars'*. Their sentence was two years in a Borstal. The *Chronicle* sent the boys on their way with the hope that they would *'benefit by the training they are to undergo, and that the result of this case will also be a warning to other young people who may be tempted to drive someone else's motor car around and to think it is a right thing to do'*.

There is little sign of depression in this picture from the Essex Show of 1928, but the county's agriculture was already slipping into crisis

Old beliefs seem to have lingered in some surprising parts of the county. It might not come as a shock to learn that cures, superstitions, sayings and unorthodox beliefs lived on in the villages of Essex, but on 3rd January 1930 the *Chronicle* detailed a story of witchcraft and its practice from Romford. The case had involved a man seeking help for his sick wife from a local who he believed to be a **'good witch'**.

Other beliefs that we might blanch at today were also current, and indeed were expressed freely by the newspaper and by others. Take, for example, the report of the trial of a young Ipswich man for theft. In his sentencing, the Judge highlighted the boy's low intellect and the fact that **'The boy's sister was in a public asylum, and there was insanity on both the father's and mother's side'**. This was a time when the belief in eugenics, the theory that traits as varied as mental illness, criminality and even poverty could be inherited, had many subscribers, not only in Nazi Germany. The Judge went on to condemn the boy as **'a victim of terrible laxity in the marriage laws. His ancestors apparently had been contributing for generations to the feeble-minded population in an appalling fashion.'** For him and many others the answer was simple: **'He [the Judge] hoped the day is not far distant when the country will either consider a measure of segregation in colonies or a properly guarded system of sterilisation, so as to save it from the awful curse which results from the inter-marriage of people of insane mind.'**

1930

Three men recount their contrasting experiences of the long hard years of the early 1930s. John Hewitt (born 1904) recalls unemployment in Chelmsford and the problems faced by families on the 'dole'. Frank Blandon (born 1905) speaks of the way in which, as a 'workless' man, he found harsh treatment at the hands of officialdom. Finally, Harold King (born 1907), a civil engineer, recalls the use of unemployed labour on the building of Colchester's by-pass.
TO LISTEN SELECT CD TRACK 3

Of all episodes in the history of twentieth century Essex, World War Two has drawn most attention. Books abound on the subject, recalling aspects of the county's part in the nation's land, sea and air struggles, as well as life at home with its images of bombing raids, Anderson shelters, gas masks, blackouts, rationing, land girls and GIs. Much has also been written about the end of the war, recording the celebrations that greeted VE-Day in May 1945 and VJ-Day in the following August. But here our focus is a new one. By February and March of 1945 it was obvious that the war was soon to be over and a new mood was coming over Essex. For the first time in nearly six years, people could look to the future, safe in the knowledge that they could begin to make plans. One word on everyone's lips, was 'reconstruction'...

1945 WAR, THE FINAL MONTHS: 'this time there is hope'

BY EARLY FEBRUARY 1945, the *Essex Chronicle* was carrying the news that Russian troops were now *'within sixty-five miles of East Berlin'*, while Allied forces were steadily approaching the Rhine to the West. After the dark days of the blitz and the false dawn of the Dunkirk landings, the *Chronicle* at last felt confident enough to declare that **'Certainly the last chapter in this long and tragic tale is now being written'**.

However, this recognition did not mean people could relax. The war effort had been a total one, and while men fought on foreign battle fronts, those left at home also played vital roles in running a wartime economy. In short, although triumph was in sight, this was no time to slacken the struggle.

PROPAGANDA

Newspapers had formed a central part in maintaining the war effort. Throughout every page of the wartime *Chronicle*, through the reports of war news, the feature articles and even the advertisements, the paper carried morale-boosting propaganda designed to help the push for victory. For example, each week's issue contained a line-drawing of an Essex scene. Entitled **'The Dear Homeland'**, the illustration was nearly always of the countryside, of historic buildings, a picture-book scene of calm and tranquillity. The message was an obvious one; this was the England that all were fighting to preserve. This was the England that should inspire the heart of every Essex man and woman.

Operating under the strict controls of the Ministry of Information, the *Chronicle* like other local newspapers became a crucial wartime news carrier

Images which combined tradition, countryside and home provided a common rallying call in wartime propaganda

The Dear Homeland . . . . . *By Adam Horne*

This week's sketch shows Newland Hall, Roxwell, which according to Wright's History of Essex belonged to King Harold before the Conquest. For the past 40 years the Menhinick family have resided there.

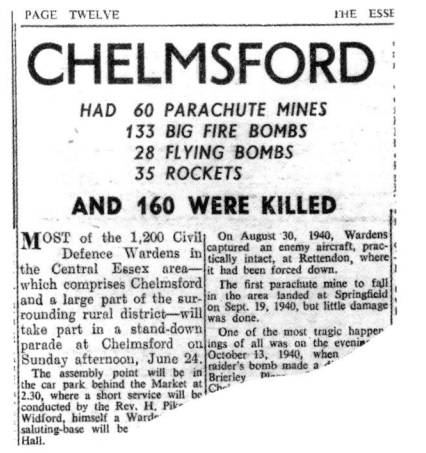

Only at the end of the war was the Chronicle able to release full details of the damaging air raids of the previous five and a half years

CHELMSFORD
HAD 60 PARACHUTE MINES
133 BIG FIRE BOMBS
28 FLYING BOMBS
35 ROCKETS
AND 160 WERE KILLED

MOST of the 1,200 Civil Defence Wardens in the Central Essex area—which comprises Chelmsford and a large part of the surrounding rural district—will take part in a stand-down parade at Chelmsford on Sunday afternoon, June 24.

The assembly point will be in the car park behind the Market at 2.30, where a short service will be conducted by the Rev. H. Pike, Widford, himself a Warden. saluting-base will be Hall.

On August 30, 1940, Wardens captured an enemy aircraft, practically intact, at Rettendon, where it had been forced down.

The first parachute mine to fall in the area landed at Springfield on Sept. 19, 1940, but little damage was done.

One of the most tragic happenings of all was on the evening October 13, 1940, when raider's bomb made a Brierley...

Glamour and contact with young men were used as a strong selling point by the NAAFI in their recruitment campaigns

HELP to cheer the boys on their way

On Miss Naffy's ready shoulders falls yet another task. When the boys come home on leave, no effort is spared to ease the burden of the journey. As the men speed homeward, Naafi girls on the leave trains serve tea and snacks in special buffet cars.

And when leave is over, soldiers and airmen again find Miss Naffy waiting to serve them, not only on the trains but in bright and cheerful canteens in the special transit camps where the men pause before returning overseas.

End-of-leave can be a grey and sombre period. Naafi has provided extra comforts and amenities to bring gaiety to the waiting hours. But their efforts will be useless without a small army of Naafi girls to provide an eager service, to cheer and encourage the boys going back and give them a parting memory of comfort and goodwill to sustain them in the days ahead.

If you are free to volunteer for this vital work, call (stating your preference for Naafi) at your local Employment Exchange. They will give you full details of this service.

serve with NAAFI
The official canteen organisation for H.M. Forces
Navy, Army & Air Force Institutes, Ruxley Towers, Claygate, Esher, Surrey

---

for central government. Press restrictions meant that people in the county were given few details of the successful strikes of the enemy. Bombing raids, for example, often went unreported altogether, while others were covered in scant and hazy detail, with phrases like *'a V-bomb fell recently in a Southern England hamlet, a row of wooden cottages was practically demolished and an inn was extensively damaged'*. It was only with the end of the war that the full facts were told of the factories and homes bombed, and of the lives lost.

By contrast, the *Chronicle* was much more precise in its appeals to readers for their assistance in the war effort. In early 1945 the Government's new 'Good Neighbour Campaign' was launched, with a full backing of publicity from the paper. Appeals were made to *'every householder to give some article from their home to help to furnish the new homes of those who have lost their possessions by bombing since January 1944 as a thanks offering from those who have to those who have not'*. Other appeals asked for people to make savings. Sometimes this meant saving money through schemes such as the wartime National Savings Certificates. But saving also referred to a long list of goods including food, waste paper, petrol, electricity, coal and scrap metal. Even if the end of the war was close, recruitment also remained as a pressing issue. Although the appeals for men willing to fight had now ceased, the calls for civilians to join the auxiliary services continued with some urgency. Young women were particular targets. The main advertisers, the NAAFI (Navy, Army and Air Force Institutes) played shamelessly and skilfully on the glamour, the contact with young men and opportunity to *'cheer and encourage the boys'* that war service would bring with it.

But the image of a united home front, of all doing their bit in the war, could not fully hide the existence of a darker side. For a start, there were the weekly columns recording the deaths of young men *'on active service'*. These were not as full as they had been in World War One, yet they were a constant reminder of the true cost of war. Then there were the frequent reports of theft and dealing in rationed goods, which suggest that a vibrant black market was operating in Essex. Typical of many reports in the *Chronicle* at this time was that of a man arrested at South Woodham Ferrers *'on a charge of receiving tinned beans, syrup, jam, milk, butter and margarine, believed to be the property of the Army authorities. P.C. Pepper gave evidence of finding the articles in the defendant's house. They included a whole cheese, which was*

38 HEADLINE HISTORY

behind a door in the living-room'. It seems that, whatever the state of the war economy, almost anything was available to those prepared to pay.

Nevertheless, these last few months of war had their more hopeful side. Advertisers promoted their products in the expectation that the peacetime economy would eventually bring an easing to rationing and a boom in consumer spending. Even if the consumer might not have much money in his or her pocket now, competition for advertising space was still fierce, as companies were keen to get their product in the public eye, hoping for longer term dividends. The biscuit manufacturers Huntley and Palmer accompanied regretful messages that their product was *'now only available in London, Southern, South Western and South Wales Food Areas'*, with the promise that *'Peace will bring increased supplies of your old favourites'*. Advertisements from British Buses carried a similar message; by showing loyalty now, customers would enjoy their reward in the future: *'In the darker days of the war, long-distance bus and coach services had to be suspended because of the vital need to conserve fuel and rubber. The public were asked to accept the accompanying discomfort and inconvenience as a contribution to the war effort. The war is not yet over, but it won't - it can't - be long before the omnibus companies restore the services, once again to play an important part in the nation's life'*.

ULTRA-MODERN FUTURE

Other advertisers saw the potential for new markets once peace was declared. Many of these advertisements were aimed directly at women, offering them a vision of how their households might soon look and operate. Electricity, and the vacuum cleaners, lights, cookers and heating that it powered, epitomised this ultra-modern future. *'You'll want comfort, cleanliness and efficiency in your peace-time home - Electricity will give you all you need'* is how The County of London Electric Supply Company appealed to readers, along with its images of women using electric irons and stoves. While its rival, the East Anglian Electric Supply Company, called on *'A Million Angry Women who are fed up with household drudgery, who want their housework mechanised'*. The message to these women was clear; they should demand electrical appliances.

It was not just advertisers who were looking forward; the people of Essex too were thinking about how post-war reconstruction was to take place. If the war had had tragic consequences, loved ones lost, cherished homes and buildings destroyed, then it also offered a new start, a chance to build a new and better society. By February 1945, the articles and letters pages of the *Chronicle* were buzzing with hopes for the future. Babies and children seem to feature in every issue of the paper, symbolising the regeneration process which was just beginning. Essex was witnessing a growing birth rate and this was trumpeted as a source of great pride, with headlines like *'More Babies than for 18 Years'* and *'Bonnie Babies by the Thousand'*, which reported on the *'remarkably high standard of health among the great majority of the mothers; and after more than five years of war and its worries. That means stronger babies too.'*

There were other signs of this new mood. If, against the odds, Britain could defeat the might of Germany, then it seemed as if any problem could now be overcome. Labour relations, for example, had long been a source of conflict and unrest. But the war had meant that employers and workers had had to work together, putting the animosity of the inter-war years to one side. Now the *Chronicle* predicted a bright future. *'We have got to live together'* it exclaimed, *'Why not try to live happily? The worker, when you get to know him, is a fine man. If employers and workers can get together and*

Electricity was supposed to represent every housewife's dream (above). East Anglian Electricity warned of the consequences if they were to be denied (below)

MARCHING HOME!

March 1945. Men of the Essex Regiment arriving home in Southend

understand each other, then we shall have a real sort of national entity...This time there is hope, thank God, and plenty of it'.

At Chelmsford another sort of future was being envisaged. Here, an Area Planning Group had been established, and at well-attended public meetings it discussed a range of plans, such as a scheme incorporating both a *'special aerodrome for civilian traffic'* and *'a riverside parkway through the town'*. But it was the urgent need to provide homes for those who had lost houses in bombing raids which created most debate. A growing call came for the founding of new towns, planned communities which could be built from scratch with homes, shops and industry, avoiding the old problems of overcrowding and congestion. Margaretting and Ongar were the early preferred suggestions as sites for development.

MORE BABIES than for 18 YEARS

Babies were a popular motif in the final months of the war, symbolising both the health of the nation and hope for the future

Other people were less concerned with the positioning of new homes than they were about their design and construction. A steady stream of letters to the *Chronicle* called for ***'homes fit for heroes'***, made of good materials and to good design, with inside bathrooms, toilets and electricity. A reader wrote deploring the building which had followed the First World War, which he labelled ***'drab, with a consistent monotony of design'*** and pleaded with architects not to make the same mistakes again, but instead ***'use their imaginations and produce something that is a credit to their profession'***.

However, the changes brought about by the war and the changes to come were not welcomed by all. For some, the brave new world others were busy planning spelled an era of lost standards, moral decay and the destruction of the good old ways. ***'In my boyhood days'***, read one letter to the newspaper, ***'almost everyone dressed in their best clothes on Sunday, and went to church. Every boy and girl I knew went to Sunday School. Juvenile crime was unknown...Our young women were modest and ladylike, only harlots painted their faces, and the only women who smoked tobacco were gypsies.'*** Another bemoaned the modern world which had emerged from the war: ***'Blame the parents, blame the mothers, blame the women who make a drunken woman fashionable, instead of physically repulsive, blame the men who teach the girls to drink, who entice them with their money and the promise of adventure, blame the cinema and its sickening glamorisation of vice, its fantastically stupid travesty of adventure in its gun-men and molls'***.

Looking back now, it is difficult to imagine why there was this level of concern. Essex cinemas, for example, places which apparently dealt out daily doses of the ***'sickening glamorisation of vice'***, were screening film classics such as 'Double Indemnity', and others with titles such as 'Gypsy Wildcat', 'Till We Meet Again' and 'The Merry Monahans'. Today it seems difficult to imagine these as being sources of depravity. And indeed, for most Essex people in 1945, the cinema was simply a place of escape, a place to forget the struggles of the war for a few hours, and perhaps, a place in which to dream about the future.

Sporting success for Essex has not always come easily. Beyond a cricket team who were all-conquering in the late 1970s and 1980s, and the individual efforts of one or two Olympic athletes, the county has had relatively little to celebrate. In football, the story has often been one of valiant struggle, but modest achievement. Even the London club of West Ham United, which holds the hearts of many Essex people, has had a habit of offering high expectation with little reward. But for a few brief weeks in 1948 Essex football did enjoy a level of success which brought it to the nation's attention and which gripped the back-page headlines. It was then that the F.A. Cup offered the backdrop against which Colchester United were to become one of the most talked about 'giant killing' teams of all time...

1948 THE GREAT CUP RUN: 'oyster-boys'

THE 1947-48 SEASON began like any other for Colchester United. They found themselves outside the 'big-time' of professional football and amidst the hum-drum existence of the Southern League. The club also had financial worries. Since 1945 its wage bill had spiralled, as the majority of players left amateur status to accept a wage for their efforts on a Saturday afternoon.

The F.A. Cup offered the one chance to escape this struggle each season, at least for a while. Every year the cup promised a brief taste of glory to one or two minor teams who could overcome the early rounds and then lose bravely to one of football's more notable sides, such as Arsenal, Manchester United or Blackpool. And with glory came something equally important: money.

1947-48 looked good for Colchester. They had already beaten bitter local rivals Chelmsford City in the first round and then overcome Banbury in the second. Their next challenge came in the shape of Wrexham. It was December, and United hoped against hope for an early, lucrative Christmas present.

Football today is often said to be driven solely by its finances. Clubs and players are said to care more for their bank accounts than for their sport. But the *Essex Chronicle* discussed Colchester's exploits in that 1947-48 season, as much in terms of balance sheets, as it did in terms of team sheets. Looking forward to the Wrexham game, the newspaper speculated, **'Their chances of entering yet another round are very good. If that happens, they will find themselves among the really big soccer and - more importantly at present - the really big money.'** It was reported that the two previous cup matches at United's Layer Road ground had produced gates of 10,000 each time, leaving a clear profit of **'£400 a match'**. A victory against Wrexham promised further riches, estimated by the *Chronicle* at **'anything up to £1,000'**.

The match was won one-nil. A glow of financial happiness spread through the Colchester United directors. Their thankfulness even extended to the players, who they entertained with **'a slap-up dinner, at which each member**

F.A. Cup: Third Round

Saturday, January 10th, 1948

Colchester United
v.
Huddersfield Town

Souvenir Programme

PRICE SIXPENCE

> **Look Around** .... **with R. A. F. Handley**
>
> # Cup-fever grips 16,000
>
> ## HUDDERSFIELD MANAGER SAYS: "I'LL GIVE YOU THE RESULT—ON SATURDAY NIGHT!"
>
> SOCCER fans are in the deadly grip of Cup-tie fever. 2.15 to-morrow afternoon is zero-hour for big-time football in Essex. Dead on the dot the £50,000 Huddersfield team will run on to the pitch at Layer Road, Colchester, with every intention of showing the United how football SHOULD be played. The oyster-boys for their part are determined not to be overshadowed by the Northern giants. Every one of the 16,000 tickets has gone. Latecomers are left clamouring for more. Extra police are being drafted... the crowds. Whe...
>
> Ted Fenton said on Wednesday: "I hope to play him—but only if he is 100 per cent. fit. We cannot take any risk and we shall not know until the last minute. Deputy-goalkeeper La Mare has been told to "stand by."
>
> Here are some brief points of interest about some of the Colchester men.
>
> All are professionals...

Essex Chronicle 9th January 1948

of the team was presented with a cheque for £10 from the Supporter's Club'.

However, the road to greater rewards was guarded by a mighty challenge. Huddersfield Town F.C., their challengers in the next round, had won the cup in the pre-war years and still graced the League's First Division. No one, it seemed, could offer much hope to United. The *Chronicle* wished the side well, but thought there was little prospect of victory: *'So here is good-luck to the big-hearted "little fellas" of Essex, who have done so well to uphold the County, and now face tough opposition. The ball will certainly need to bounce right every time.'* Even their supporters gave them little chance, as one told the paper *'I think the United may be able to hold them - with luck - for the first thirty minutes...After that, well, they would do well if they lost by only five goals.'* Only the Huddersfield manager failed to share this opinion, his words hinting at what was to come. As his players prepared confidently with rounds of golf at Frinton, he spoke darkly, in terms which even then must have been clichéd, predicting that *'strange things happen in football'*.

FAMOUS VICTORY

The 16,000 people crammed into Colchester's Layer Road that day in January 1948 witnessed a famous one-nil victory for United. The only thing tighter-packed than the crowd seems to have been the Colchester defence, which the *Chronicle* described as *'oyster-like with relentless tackling'*. R.A.F. Handley, the *Chronicle's* sports writer, showed little compassion for the defeated Huddersfield team and their supporters. His after-match reports from the two teams' dressing rooms make for contrasting reading. Amongst the home team he found *'players leaping up and down, with broad smiles, hand-shaking and back slapping'*. While amongst their opponents he discovered the expensive star player, Peter Doherty, with a *'dazed expression on his face...He stood naked in the dressing room as I spoke to him. He shook his head and made no excuses for his astonishing failure. Somehow a man never looks worth £10,000 in his birthday suit.'* Throughout, Handley also took great delight in calling Huddersfield *'the northerners'*, ending his report with the claim that *'Colchester was a first-class town way back before Hudders was even a field'*.

The next round gave Colchester yet another tie at home, this time against more northern opposition in the shape of Bradford City. Confidence was growing in the United camp; some supporters had even fashioned their own replica cup, ready to present to the team on their upcoming triumph. After all, Bradford were only from the Football League's Second Division, albeit that they themselves were cup 'giant-killers', having beaten the mighty Arsenal in the previous round. Only the bookmakers doubted Colchester's claims. In the town's High Street it was still possible to buy odds of 4,000 to 1 on United winning the competition.

Match-day started early for the 1,500 Bradford supporters who, having travelled all night by chartered coaches, arrived in Colchester creating quite a stir. *'The ancient garrison town was number one whoopee spot gone crazy on Saturday. Bradford supporters danced in the streets, hunted noisily for breakfast and a barber, and sang their battle hymn, "On Ilkla' Moor"...Barrow boys were out selling rosettes with the Colchester colours. A man wearing an opera hat sold balloons. It was gala day'*. But for Bradford fans, like those of Huddersfield before them, it was to be a wasted journey, because despite going one-nil down after just fifteen minutes, United powered back to triumph three-two.

In the days following the victory, the true extent of Colchester's achievement was realised. They had reached the last sixteen of the F.A. Cup, the first time a non-league side had done so since 1911. Their next challenge was to be their greatest yet, away to First Division Blackpool. But this was no cause for depression. At a time when people were struggling with post-war austerity, the affect on the town's morale was tangible: *'What the U's have done for Colchester might be estimated in saved doctor's bills! Frowns have disappeared, new life lights up tired faces, and one topic - football - dominates all others. People greet each other with "Up the U's" with an animation usually foreign to the restrained English nature'*.

Ted Fenton, Colchester United's player-manager, proved to be an astute publicist as well as a good match tactician

ESSEX CHRONICLE

No. 9,566   TELEPHONES: CHELMSFORD 4631-2   FRIDAY, 23rd JANUARY, 1948.   BRAINTREE 408   Price TWOPENCE

EXCITEMENT RISES OVER TOMORROW'S GREAT F.A. CUP MATCH
COLCHESTER HAVE 50-50 CHANCE

VOICE of Probably no other game in tomorrow's F.A. Cup-ties has captured the imagination more than the much publicised match between Colchester United, Cup giant-killers, and Bradford, the Second ... team which also caused ...

Once again, alongside the glory stood the cool realisation that money was to be made from success. *'Colchester has a team worth £50,000 to the town'* reported the *Chronicle*. *'That is a conservative estimate of the value of publicity gained by United since they started their run. Now that's a whale of a lot of green 'uns. And do you notice the subtle campaign for the native oysters that's going on? "Our team won because they were fed on Colchester oysters" or "the Council say they will go on feeding the team on oysters"...A smart lot of boys, these Colcestrians. Getting every ounce of thrills and fun from their team, they are at the same time enjoying their commercial value. And who can blame them?'*

STRONG WOMAN

It was now that the oyster boy's exploits were drawing national attention. There were to be no less that five newsreel film companies ready with cameras as the Colchester players ran out on to the Blackpool pitch, along with radio commentators scrutinising their every move from the stands. Much of the pre-match interest was to focus upon United's player-manager, Ted Fenton. In an 'exclusive' interview with the ex-West Ham player, the *Essex Chronicle* described him as *'the most talked of man in the country this week...certainly no film star has more admirers'*. But behind every manager, it seems, there needed to be a strong woman. *'How many of us,'* asked the *Chronicle*'s reporter without a hint of irony, *'are giving a thought to the little woman who is responsible for Ted's success - Ted's wife...Petite, with dark hair and blue eyes and a charmingly frank manner, little Mrs Fenton is thirty-two years of age...Mrs Fenton devotes her life to Ted and their two children...It is Mrs Fenton's job to keep Ted fighting fit, but she is not entitled to any extras*

Media attention even led to a cartoon chronicle of the life of the Colchester United manager

because of this. His rations are the same as everyone else's, and she has to use all her ingenuity to keep him strong and well...Mrs Fenton says the Colchester United team do not go in for gland treatment or any of the temporary stimulants which at one time became the fashion in some places. Ted does not even have cod liver oil to keep him warm.'

With this kind of support behind them it seemed that Colchester must have a good chance of victory. Indeed, pre-match predictions were now more optimistic than they had been against Huddersfield. Fenton told the press that he had a secret plan which would have the opposition *'floundering in the middle of the Black-pool'*, and of his firm belief that *'Colchester would win'*.

However, this time it was not to be. Perhaps Colchester had been cursed with bad luck before they even set foot on the field of play. The *Chronicle* believed so: *'Who has ever heard of THIRTEEN players travelling together on the eve of an important cup-tie. Yet that is what Colchester United has done. Thirteen faces full of confidence and oysters, beamed from railway carriages.'* But more likely, it was because the brave non-league team had come up against a top-class professional side containing such post-war stars as Stanley Matthews and Stan Mortensen. In front of what must have seemed a vast and intimidating crowd of 30,000 people the *'oyster-boys'* sank to a five-nil defeat.

The end of what had been a glorious and lucrative cup-run had come swiftly and cruelly. Players, management and supporters returned to the less-glamorous life of a struggling non-league side. After all, within a week United were due to play yet another important game, but this time against the less than mighty opposition provided by Lowestoft Town F.C.

Essex Chronicle 5th February 1948

1948

Arthur Turner (born 1921) played as a forward in Colchester United's dramatic cup run. Here he recounts some of his earliest memories of playing football in the streets around his home on the Isle of Dogs. We also hear of his signing with Charlton Athletic aged sixteen, the nature of footballing fame, the great players of his day and the experience of playing in the FA Cup Final of 1946. He then remembers the Colchester team that he joined in 1947, the end of their cup run against the mighty Blackpool and the disappointment of defeat. In the final excerpts Arthur also tells of the physical nature of football after the war, the ability that he possessed and compares today's stars with those of the past.

TO LISTEN SELECT CD TRACK 4

Look Around .... with R. A. F. Handle

This will shake the superstitious:

Thirteen players went to Blackpool!

And the Mayors exchanged greetings

WHO has ever heard of THIRTEEN players travelling together on the eve of an important Cup-tie? Yet that is what Colchester United F.C. has done. Thirteen faces, full of confidence and oysters, beamed from the carriages of the 10.50 from Euston yesterday morning as it steamed out heading for Blackpool. Hundreds of telegrams wishing them luck have arrived at the Layer Road ground. The Mayor of Blackpool has invited Councillor Dansie, J.P., Mayor of Colchester, to spend the week-end as his guest at Blackpool. Sporting Alderman Arthur Andrews, Mayor of Chelmsford, has written to Colches-

Planner Fenton returned fr[om] watching the Northerners p[lay] on Saturday. He reckons latest plan will leave Stanle[y's] boys floundering in the middle [of] the Black-pool. He is cautiou[s] but quite confident that Colch[es]ter will again stand the footb[all] pool forecasts on their hea[ds.] For anyone wanting to mark th[eir] coupons, Ted Fenton tells [us] "Colchester will win."

• Jock Duncan, Layer Ro[ad] groundsman, says the pitch [at] Blackpool is more sandy th[an] muddy, and very little differe[nce]

With its miles of salt-marsh, mud filled creeks and shingle beaches, Essex has always had a close relationship with the sea. From oyster fishermen at Burnham to barge skippers at Maldon, from boat builders at Wivenhoe to leisure boat captains at Southend, many Essex people have drawn a living from it, while countless others have drawn pleasure. Yet the relationship has not always been a benign one, for during the night of Saturday 31st January 1953, Essex witnessed another side to the sea's presence. With a power which was irresistible, and a speed that was startling, it overtook sea defences that had been built over centuries. Some people woke to find the water advancing with icy stealth towards their homes, leaving them barely the time to save themselves and a few possessions. Others found even this last minute flight impossible; the sea was upon them. For them there was to be no escape from this tide...

1953 THE FLOODS: 'the night when the monster came'

A VISIT FROM the sea had been expected that Saturday night. Earlier in the day notices had been relayed to east coast ports and warnings given of **'an abnormally high tide'**. But these had created no undue panic. After all, the flat and exposed Essex coast was used to some regular flooding. Since the Second World War there had been sixty similar warnings, each one acting as a brief reminder of the power and potential of the sea. But none had inflicted much damage beyond a few flooded fields and waterlogged basements.

THE COMING DISASTER

However, this time things were to be different, as the high sea was swollen by exceptionally strong winds which drove it towards the shore. But as the tide came in, rising inch-by-inch, people went about their business, oblivious to the coming disaster. At Canvey Island, the scene of so much of the destruction which was to come, people were preoccupied with enjoying a function at the Memorial Hall, newly opened that day in honour of those that had served in the last war. At Southend, couples danced in the pier's ballroom. While at Clacton, families were enjoying a night at the theatre.

Only at Harwich, which sees the earliest tide in Essex, were signs of approaching trouble spotted. Here, at 9.20pm, the Harbour Master left his office to peer across the mouths of the Stour and Orwell estuaries towards Felixstowe. What he saw alarmed him, for the tide was already up to its predicted high water mark, yet it still had three and half hours to flow. By 10pm the tide had begun to flood the quay. Harwich police telephoned a warning to their Chelmsford headquarters. Further down the coast, drivers crossing The Strood causeway to Mersea Island began to notice the thin layer

---

TIDE TABLE
HIGH WATER AT SOUTHEND AND BURNHAM-ON-CROUCH

FEB		a.m.	p.m.
6 FRIDAY	.. ..	4.15 ..	4.44
7 SATURDAY	.. ..	4.54 ..	5.27
8 SUNDAY	.. ..	5.36 ..	6.24
9 MONDAY	.. ..	7.01 ..	7.44
10 TUESDAY	.. ..	8.40 ..	9.15
11 WEDNESDAY	..	10.04 ..	10.28
12 THURSDAY	..	11.08 ..	11.25

Clacton and Walton-on-Naze about 30 minutes earlier and Maldon about 10 minutes later than above times.

LIGHTING-UP TIME
Fri., Feb. 6, 5.28; Sat., 7, 5.29; Sun., 8, 5.31; Mon., 9, 5.33; Tues., 10, 5.34; Wed., 11, 5.36; Thurs., 12, 5.38.

Canvey lies swamped in the flood's aftermath

Air scene of tragedy
Half - submerged Canvey Island from the air. Buses, run as far as possible on the island, were used to evacuate residents to Benfleet.—Picture by Evening Standard cameraman Victor Drees.

of water beneath their wheels. By 10.30pm the island was cut off. At the same time, the promenade at Maldon began to disappear from view, while at Walton-on-the-Naze waves were beginning to swamp the sea-front.

Soon after 11pm policemen in Harwich were running between houses attempting to rouse families, warning them of the worsening situation. But within minutes waves were breaking on sea-front properties, sending ice cold salt water through the narrow streets of the Old Town. The town hall and fire station were both quickly flooded, along with pubs, shops and houses. People were to speak later of the water *'crashing through front doors'*, belittling the attempts of those who tried to stop it.

As people in Harwich struggled to save themselves and their possessions, some thirty-five miles away Fred Leach sat in his farmhouse kitchen, close to

Caravans at Canvey. Essex Chronicle 6th February 1953

the sea wall at Canvey Island. At 11.50pm his telephone began to ring. It was unusual to get a call so late, even if it was a Saturday evening. Telling his story later to the *Essex Chronicle*, Fred recalled that the voice on the other end of the line was that of a panicking engineer from the Essex River Board at Upminster, warning him of a *'freak high tide and flooding'*. Within minutes Fred was examining the bridge which stood close to his farm, and which formed Canvey's only link with the mainland. It was then as he stood there **'that the swirling sea came over the bridge and lapped over his boots, creeping down the road'**.

By 11.59pm Fred had got back to the house and was telephoning the town's police station. He spoke breathlessly to the desk sergeant. **'It was the first news the police had received.'** At 12.03am Fred **'rushed to a row of nearby cottages and awakened the farm workers and their families. Several of the men raced across fields to the houses fringing the main town, crying warnings as they ran. Most of the people awoke to find the lower parts of their houses already swimming in sea water'**. Fred then returned to evacuate his own family from the farmhouse, just in time, for at 12.05am, the sea burst over, completely flooding the main road and surrounding farmland. Within minutes the town was also under several feet of water.

NIGHT TIME DESTRUCTION

For the next two hours before the tide began to ebb, the sea held sway. From Harwich and Manningtree in the north, to West Ham and Tilbury in the south, communities along the coastline of Essex were submerged. In the dark confusion of that night fleeing family members were parted from one another, people went unaccounted for, or were lost, while houses and possessions were abandoned in the scramble for dry ground and safety. It was only with the daybreak that a full sense of the night-time destruction emerged. In total, the sea defences had been breached in 300 places, flooding some 30,000 acres, taking the lives of 119 people and making a further 21,000 people homeless.

The *Essex Chronicle* was quickly on the scene, relaying the images and stories of the tragedy to the rest of the county. Its coverage concentrated on the

At Goldhanger the sea penetrated a mile inland, flooding valuable farm land with salt water

Emergency vehicles wait at the edge of Canvey Island's flood waters

Much of the east coast was affected

At Benfleet little Derek Storey, rescued from the floods, was being cared for by Miss Jean Gatward at a rest centre in a school building.

two places worst hit: Jaywick, which had seen 35 deaths and 600 of its remaining 700 population homeless, and Canvey Island, with 58 dead and 11,000 out of 11,500 of its people unable to return to their homes.

'Terror Sunday' was the headline which led the *Chronicle*'s description of the scene. *'The little town of Jaywick lies smashed and flooded...Many people think Jaywick is finished...The sea seems determined to keep its own'*. Quickly on the spot, the reporters' stories carry a startled, disbelieving tone at the sight of so much destruction. *'Rowing was hard work. We skirted Lamp-posts and bus stops. The tops of garden fences scraped the bottom of the boat. Cars stood in gardens...Men in little boats carried on their pathetic door-to-door hunt among the flooded bungalows, breaking windows and roofs, looking for lost relatives. In one road a bungalow stood in the centre at an angle. It had been swept from the end of the street - at least sixty yards away. It stood there, undamaged, the furniture still inside'.*

As survivors told their accounts, stories emerged of loss and of despair. Where the facts were thin then the *Chronicle* filled the gaps with detail verging on melodrama. From Canvey the newspaper reported the death of a young couple, *'caught by the dark waters that swirled over the veranda of their little home. The man tried to save his wife by carrying her pick-a-back. For that was how they were found together in their last embrace. The man, coming out of the house deep in water had slipped over with his wife on his back. And so drowned, she with him. Yet their child lived; the father had put her in a cot and she had floated away, and had been saved'.*

At Jaywick, a rescuer told of how he had come across an elderly couple while making a house-to-house search in his boat. Alone, with only their dog for comfort, the couple were trapped in the loft of their bungalow, with water flowing around them. *'They had been there for hours. He helped the man into the boat, and placed the dog on his lap'*. But just as she was about to be saved, *'the woman panicked. She slipped into the water and was swept away in a matter of seconds. There was nothing to be done'*.

For every tragic story came tales of escape, good fortune and heroism. With the war just six years past, the flood seemed to give a sense of purpose around which Essex people could come together again. The *Essex Chronicle* certainly recognised this mood. Its reporting in the weeks after the disaster took on a war-time tone, playing up the resilience of the county's people in the face of such adversity. Despite the terrible events of that night, the flood was to be seen as a time when people worked together in a common cause, *'Behind the horror of this tragic week lies a strong sense of achievement. A story of volunteers responding in their hundreds to aid the sufferers...The disaster had many heroes. All the rescued praise the rescuers, the men who gathered their small boats like a second "Dunkirk" to help their neighbours'*. The rebuilding effort which followed seemed to show the best of Essex as *'People queued with their gifts of clothing and other articles. Local authorities all over Essex opened immediate relief funds. This catastrophe showed once again the warm hearts of Essex people, as they rallied to the call for help. From the Central Control established at the Essex County Hall, down to the smallest village depot, the same astonishing public spirit of co-operation and willing service was demonstrated'*.

The relief effort was indeed huge. Some 21,000 people had been made temporarily homeless, as the water gradually receded and houses took time to dry. Many families opened their doors to these refugees, in much the same way that they had done to accommodate war-time evacuees. Other people came forward to help repair the fractured sea defences, filling sand-bags and moving earth in what became a race to beat the next high tides. Elsewhere, countless others gave aid in small ways, donating blankets, giving up old clothing, or simply contributing a few shillings to the relief funds that were set up in nearly every community.

However, there was another, less seemly side to the flood's aftermath. For in the chaos and confusion which accompanied the flood and its after-effects, a few took the opportunity to exploit its victims. Within three weeks of the disaster the *Essex Chronicle* ran the headline *'Canvey Homes Looted'* above a report which told its readers, *'Many flood victims, returning for the first time to their homes at Canvey Island and Jaywick, are finding that looters have arrived first. Among the thousands of honest helpers who have done so much, a few have taken advantage...it is a fact that some of the thieving has been committed by "volunteers", under the guise of "defence work"...Almost as soon as the floods began petty thieves were making their way to the areas, breaking into deserted homes and helping themselves'*. For some, the temptation of unguarded homes had proved too strong.

Nevertheless, life and normality was quickly restored to the Essex coast. February was blessed by some unseasonably fine weather, while the patched up sea defences held firm against the tides. Within days of the flood people began to return home. Many found houses which still stood ankle deep in brackish muddy water. The *Chronicle* declared that ***'The great dry-out is on! Over the fences and garden walls hang mattresses, bolsters, rugs and carpets. The furniture is airing in the gardens. The shops are open again. People are sitting at morning coffee in the tea-shops.'*** But if life had been restored, it could never quite be the same again. For a few, brief hours on the night of Saturday, 31st January 1951 salt water had colonised the coast-lands of Essex. All those who came back to resume their lives at places like Jaywick, Wallasea, Foulness, Canvey and Tilbury did so in the knowledge that they dwelt next to what the *Essex Chronicle* now called the ***'monster'***. From the seaside bungalows and shanties, with names like 'Peacehaven' and 'Dunroamin', with their colourful exteriors and pretty seashell edged flower-beds, the survivors of the flood now looked out with suspicious eyes across the deep, dark expanse of the sea.

Stepping in to trouble: part of the police's anti-looting squad detailed to the Essex coast

1953

Donald Payne (born 1930) came with his mother to Canvey Island aged three. Here he recalls the island before the war and the primitive conditions of its housing. His wife, Thelma (born 1931), recounts the story of their meeting and falling in love. Together the couple settled in a bungalow on the island and in January 1953 were looking forward to the arrival of their first child. It was then that the flood struck. The Paynes recall that tragic night, their escape, the looters who scavenged from deserted homes and the long legacy for the returning community.

TO LISTEN SELECT CD TRACK 5

The great flood of February 1953 represented a significant setback in the ongoing task of rebuilding Essex after 1945. Homes destroyed, evacuees needing housing, uncertainty about the future, all brought back uncomfortable memories of the war years. Yet 1953 also offered a chance for the people of Essex to look forward and try to envisage the future. The previous year had seen the death of their king, George VI, and now a new monarch had come to the throne. Elizabeth was young, just twenty-six at the time of her father's death. She also had a young family with two infant children. The combination of her youth, and the desire amongst people in general to look forward and cast aside the austerity of the war, gave the Coronation on 2nd June special poignancy. At the time there was talk of the emergence of a new age, the age of Elizabeth, and expectations were high...

1953 DAWN OF A NEW ELIZABETHAN AGE: 'we are proud and humble, strong and gentle'

IN THE APPROACH to Coronation Day the *Essex Chronicle* was unstinting in its patriotism and unashamedly brazen in its use of the event as an opportunity for self-publicity. Advertising its 'Coronation Special Issue' to its readers, it talked of plans to provide its **'large family of readers'** with 32 pages dedicated to the **'best presentation of pictures and news'**, an issue which represented **'the highest number of pages in our long history, which extends over nearly 200 years and seven Coronations'**.

Readers were not to be disappointed. The Coronation edition carried stories and pictures of the celebrations from across Essex. Alongside this, it also attempted to introduce a more serious note in its coverage. For the crowning of a new queen was not simply an opportunity for a breather from the task of rebuilding the nation. Instead, it was seen as a key component of that rebuilding process. After generations raised certain in the knowledge of the nation's international power, post war Britain was now less assured, perhaps less secure in what it meant to be British. After all, it was just six years since it had lost India to independence, and with it one of the last of its great colonial

32-Page Coronation Events and Essex Show Souvenir

Essex Chronicle

No. 9,847 Telephone: CHELMSFORD 4631/2   FRIDAY, JUNE 12, 1953   Price THREEPENCE

AS THE PREMIER COUNTY NEWSPAPER WHICH IS TO-DAY REPORTING THE CLIMAX TO ITS SEVENTH CORONATION AND HAS FAITHFULLY SERVED A WIDE READERSHIP IN NINE REIGNS, WE HAVE THE GREAT HONOUR AND PRIVILEGE TO ACCLAIM

QUEEN ELIZABETH II

possessions. If nothing else, the Coronation appeared to give an opportunity to take stock and secure a national purpose for the future.

'Behind all the celebrations there will be a note of thanksgiving to God and prayers for the Queen's glorious reign' was how the *Chronicle* introduced this message to its readers. Later editions of the newspaper spoke of *'never, surely, in our long history, has the nation been so united in its affection for the Royal Family as now'* and that *'beneath the splendour and the majesty lies simplicity, faith, and strong family ties. With that backing the Throne will last.'* For the *Chronicle*, the Coronation was not simply a day of celebration, but an opportunity for the nation to reassert its influence. News and pictures of the event would *'spread round the world like a girdle of charm, a fairy tale come true, a fairy tale for young and old, for black and*

Coronation carnivals proved a popular way of celebrating. Here Chelmsford's carnival 'Queen', Pamela Arran, looks suitably regal

brown, for white and yellow...to show the world of what stuff we're made...that we are proud and humble, strong and gentle, the roots of our tree firm and deep in the traditions of our long heritage'.

Coronation week also brought news that a British organised expedition had become the first to conquer Everest. It seemed of little matter that it had been a Nepalese and a New Zealander who had been the ones to reach the summit. The Everest triumph appeared to confirm Britain as a world leader once more. While for the *Chronicle* it suggested a brighter future: **'Following the conquest of Everest and the general surge of renewed hope spreading across the country the Coronation is the finest tonic a war-weary nation could have.'** It was Britain that stood at the top of the world once more.

A COUNTY CELEBRATES

The people of Essex recognised this mood and produced a celebration on a scale which rivalled those that had greeted Queen Victoria's Diamond Jubilee in 1897 and V-E Day in 1945. The *Chronicle* carried reports from nearly every town and village, detailing the humblest street party and the grandest Coronation parade. In some places the day was marked in a simple style. At Black Notley, as in many other villages, the church bells were rung and Coronation mugs, hats and other memorabilia were presented to local children. At Great Bardfield an Elizabethan pageant was held. At Boreham an ox roast was enjoyed by 1,500, but only after consent was given from the Ministry of Food, for rationing was still in place. While at Braintree an open-day at the nearby Wethersfield US Air Force base left the 20,000 who visited with **'jet whine in their ears and the taste of real hot dogs in their mouths'**. Even the communities which had been submerged by the February floods used the Coronation as part of their recovery process. Canvey Island, for example, drew praise from the newspaper as its battered townspeople organised celebrations in which they could boast **'1,755 school children enjoyed tea and sports, and there was entertainment and tea for old age pensioners...followed by dancing at the War Memorial Hall'**.

TOTALLY MODERN

But alongside the 'traditional' street parties, parades, torch light processions and sports days, the Coronation spawned another style of celebration, one that had never been witnessed before. One that was totally modern. This was television.

Some celebrations were less conventional; Little Waltham's Coronation Pram 'Derby' was one such example

THE BEST—AND THE FUNNIEST- CARNIVAL EVER

Essex Chronicle 12th June 1953

56 HEADLINE HISTORY

In the weeks before the Coronation, the classified columns of the *Chronicle* began to show a mounting number of advertisements encouraging the people of Essex not to miss out on this new experience. *'Television News!!'* ran one advertisement headline, mimicking the style of a press report, **'The new 17 inch Sobell Television, in a handsome veneered cabinet, at 74 guineas, is remarkable value in new large picture television. We have good selections of the latest models, but demand for the Coronation is now exceeding the supply, and we advise you to get your TELEVISION NOW'**.

Through television's coverage of the Coronation, Essex people were able to share in a national event in a new way, which until then had been unimaginable. For example, the Diamond Jubilee of 1897 had been celebrated widely in the county, yet news of London's rejoicings and those of the rest of Britain had only reached Essex towns and villages by word of mouth and through the pages of newspapers such as the *Chronicle*. It had been several days before descriptions had reached the most distant ears and eyes. Yet 2nd June 1953 changed all this. Essex people sat down as one, not merely to hear news of the Coronation in London, but to watch it live, as if it was they who stood in the front row of the crowded Mall and who were perched upon the best seats in Westminster Abbey.

A topical float at the Witham Coronation carnival

With curtains drawn to improve the black and white pictures, many people's first experiences of television were of their Queen being crowned. Whole streets crowded around the new set of a proud neighbour. There they were plied with sandwiches and drink in one of the many private Coronation parties in Essex. Elsewhere, villages and towns such as High Ongar, Sible Hedingham, Harlow, North Fambridge and Tiptree held their own mass screenings; whole communities viewing as one. At Braintree it was reported that *'fourteen TV sets were in operation in the Corn Exchange and there were a continual stream of visitors'*. At Colchester *'Nearly 800 elderly people gathered at the Moot Hall to view the Coronation in comfort from sixteen TV sets, which were arranged in a circle'*. While even in the small village of Faulkbourne: *'125 villagers watched on a set specially installed in the village hall. It was the first time television had been seen in the village as there are no privately-owned sets.'*

STREETS DESERTED

Television, like the radio before it, was changing the face of Essex society. Until the age of mass communication large public events had brought people out of their homes, into the streets and beyond, to gather as one to celebrate, to hear worrying news, to protest, to witness sporting events, and so on. Yet during the Coronation the *Essex Chronicle* reported that in many parts of the county *'streets were practically deserted...most of the celebrations are confined to public and private TV parties'*. As private ownership of sets rapidly increased, it began to take people further and further into their own homes. From 1953 onwards, national and international events, such as England's 1966 World Cup triumph, the moon landing and the wedding of Charles and Diana, would be family affairs, afternoons and evenings in front of the 'box'.

So, the Coronation of 1953 brought with it something besides a new queen. On that June day people across Essex used the occasion to tune in to a new experience. If this moment was to signal the start of a new 'Elizabethan age', then it was also the birth of the age of television.

That was the time when...

The *Chronicle* reported on something else which was new for 1953, *'An unusual name was given to a baby girl at a baptism in Chelmsford Cathedral on Sunday afternoon. The name was Beverley...By the side of the entry of the baptism has been added 'a female child', so that those consulting the register in the future will not be confused.'*

Meanwhile, the newspaper's fashion editor was urging its female readers to recognise their own shortcomings, *'If you aren't the type to wear jeans, then don't. If your hips are a little too bulgy then don't wear a tube skirt just because it's fashionable. If your shoulders are bony, then don't display them. If your legs aren't a good feature then hide them. Just know your faults, and once you do then you are well on the way...'*

Alongside this feature ran an advertisement tempting female readers to mark the approaching national celebration by having *'A Coronation Permanent Wave, 22s 6d at Maison Marcel, Ladies Hairdressers, Chelmsford'*.

Any one looking for a new home could have bought a detached bungalow in South Woodham for £1,150, or a three bedroom house *'on a bus route'* in Billericay for £1,600.

Those seeking a completely new change of scene must have been drawn to an advertisement which read *'AUSTRALIA: an Australian Immigration representative will be at Chelmsford Employment exchange on Monday to answer enquiries about Assisted Passages to Australia. You are invited to call'*.

With the war a retreating memory, a new threat to the Essex people could be seen in an advertisement which implored, *'Join your neighbours in Civil Defence - We must be strong to preserve peace. Men and women over thirty years of age are needed immediately for the HQ section to train in reconnaissance and communications and other specialist subjects, such as radio, telephony, bacteriological, chemical, and atomic warfare'*.

On the farms and in the gardens of Essex another type of chemical warfare was beginning to be fought. *'Take the Pests out of Peas'* ran another advert. *'Spray Psylortox 167 - This DDT emulsion, specially formulated by Pest Control Ltd, will rid your peas of both pea moth and green fly.'* The results of this chemical assault on the wildlife of the county were yet to be fully understood.

1953

At the time of the Coronation in June 1953 Marcus Knight (born 1929) was working long hours for the English Electric Valve Company in Chelmsford, helping to produce the valves that would help illuminate the screens of thousands of the new television sets coming into the homes of British people. Here he recalls the excitement of Coronation day and the pride felt by those Essex people who were among the first to enter the television age.
TO LISTEN SELECT CD TRACK 6

Essex, which twenty years before was wondering how it could feed itself, was by 1963 in the midst of a consumer boom. Wartime habits of scrimping, saving, of doing without and of 'make do and mend' had been replaced with affluence and choice. The result was a revolution, one that involved changing habits and appearances. Essex was never to be the same again...

1963 A CONSUMER REVOLUTION: 'nothing but optimism and sunshine'

'*SUCCESS...SUCCESS...SUCCESS*' was the simple way in which the *Essex Chronicle* captured the state of the county's economic health that year. While admitting that there was '*growing unemployment in the North of England*', the paper told its readers gleefully that '*we are delighted to report nothing but optimism and sunshine from the South*'. Marconi, the flagship of Essex industry, was said to be leading the way with '*a record order book and factories working at full capacity*'. The *Chronicle*'s own bulging 'Situations Vacant' column testified that the county was indeed doing well.

1963 began inauspiciously with a 'big-freeze', heavy snow covering the country for much of December, January and February. But freezing temperatures could not mask a general thaw which was taking place within the British people themselves. Since the mid-1950s a new, affluent society had been emerging, with many enjoying higher wages and more disposable income. With the ending of all forms of rationing in 1954, shops could also offer more to buy. The result was a consumer revolution.

NO BOUNDARIES
The *Chronicle*'s pages during and after the war had been full of advertisements for saving money, saving fuel and saving food. Now they were full with a different message, one of how, where and on what to spend money. Allied to this were changing tastes. The birth of commercial television, rock'n'roll, the relaxation in censorship to allow the publication of *Lady Chatterley's Lover*, all had been recent milestones on the path to a new era in which the formality of old Britain was being overturned. Some in Essex bemoaned the loss of 'old-fashioned standards' and its strict morality. But many others embraced the new fashions, the growing room for self-expression, informality and a sense of freedom. Besides, the future promised greater abundance and advance in a modern world that seemed to know no boundaries to its own progress.

Horizons were beginning to shift in Essex. People were now looking beyond the county's own 'sunshine coast' to a world beyond. Recognising this growing mood, the *Chronicle* began to explore the pull of the foreign holiday on its readers. Throughout the early weeks of 1963, as people shivered at home, articles appeared which told of the lure and the attractions of a place known only as '*the Continent*':

CHELMSFORD AND DISTRICT EDITION

THE ESSEX Chronicle

198th YEAR
No. 10,345
SALES NOW EXCEED 37,600 WEEKLY
FRIDAY, JANUARY 11th, 1963
PRICE THREEPENCE

SUCCESS ..... SUCCESS ..... SUCCESS .....

SUNSHINE REPORT FROM CHELMSFORD FACTORIES

TODAY, as Lord Hailsham settles down to the difficult task of sorting out growing unemployment in the North of England, we are delighted to report nothing but optimism and sunshine from the South. Two world-famous companies—Marconi's and Crompton Parkinson—are in high spirits. Of the year just ended Marconi's say it was "highly successful with a record order...

factories working at full capacity." A £3 million contract from Ghana, announced recently, for sound and television equipment is the biggest single contract ever to be placed with the Division. From Crompton P...

well maintained and profits for the first time exceeded £3 million." Their Chelmsford factory is right in the forefront. All this, with the giant Hoffmann Manufacturing Company and English Electric Valve Company, spell PROSPERITY in mid-Essex. Particularly to the many families dependant on these great management workers

'As families spend evenings jostling for position by the fire in the worst freeze-up in living memory, a sudden warm glow invades the room...The weather is not as bad as it might be...those frozen pipes may not have burst after all...the coal supplies may last a lot longer than expected...anyway, there is always tomorrow. And in a few months' time tomorrow will be a holiday'.

The choice of holidays was tempting. High Street travel firms such as Thomas Cook, Pickfords and Cosmos were all offering the new package holidays to the sun. As little as £10 could buy a return flight from Southend airport to the Channel Islands. While 34 and 36 guineas bought 15 days by air on either the Costa Brava or in Majorca. Greece, as yet an underdeveloped destination, was far more expensive, two weeks costing £116, a large sum by the standards of 1963.

HAPPY HOLIDAYS

The alternative to air travel was, of course, the car, and the advertisements of ferry firms competed fiercely for the newspaper's space alongside those of the airlines and travel agents. Once upon *'the Continent'*, the *Essex Chronicle* advised its readers on accommodation. *'Camping'*, it explained, *'is no longer the hardy, stark pastime it was. Modern tents are spacious as caravans and the facilities on registered sites are equal to any emergency'.* Perhaps the 'emergency' it had in mind was the one linked to foreign food. It was here that the self-catering villa held significant advantages in the opinion of the *Chronicle*: *'Also popular with the motoring fraternity is the villa renting craze. By this method one can enjoy the Continental scenery but control the cuisine, sometimes an important factor in the desire to provide a happy holiday.'*

Although foreign holidays were all the fashion, the *Chronicle* also took care to remind readers that *'not everyone wants to go abroad - not everyone can afford it! And Britain is a wonderful country in its own right...'* But even here tastes were changing. For people in Essex, an annual holiday before the war was likely to have been a short and comparatively local affair; a day-trip to the seaside at Clacton, Walton or Southend being the typical choice. Now trips lasted longer and took people further afield, as paid holidays from work lengthened and people began to have more money in their pockets. So it was that the newspaper remarked that *'The West Country becomes increasingly popular with each year'*, while also advising readers that *'Holiday camps are always attractive to families and in addition to Billy Butlin's famous camps there are literally scores of others...'*

OFF THE PEG

The consumer boom even brought changes to the appearance of the county's people, altering the way that they looked. A desire to be fashionable was nothing new. But whereas once 'being with it' had meant owning a spare suit or frock for Sunday, now people's wardrobes were growing to include the new, relatively cheap and diverse 'off the peg' lines stocked by many high street shops. *'At last we are emerging from that wintry go-slow...'* the *Chronicle* told its female readers. *'There is spring in the shop windows, and how cheering it is! There are gay colours, vivid as hot summer days. We are it seems to wear high waists. And there are full circle skirts for all the world like the ones we wear for skating'*. Also in fashion was the *'new U neckline,*

By the 1960s foreign holidays were eating into the domestic leisure market. Holiday camps, like that of Butlins at Clacton, now faced growing competition

Essex Chronicle 4th January 1963

which is distinctly décolleté...' along with '...high crown hats worn tilted forward over the forehead...definitely for the very young'. For men the Chronicle's correspondent noticed that fur hats were in fashion, along with 'black velvet suits...the latest thing for the arty set'.

THE DOOR TO HAIR BEAUTY

Hairstyles were changing too. For some women a new 'hair-do' meant the modern 'Lotus Line' cut. For others it meant undergoing a 'permanent wave treatment', like the 'Clynol T.V. Wave', or the 'Vienna Alpine Wave', available for 21 shillings or 50 shillings at the latest Chelmsford salon, the thoughtfully titled '113 Rainsford Road'. The Chronicle reported from the salon with the message that *'The door to hair beauty is open...'* alongside a story of a visit there by *'the celebrated Continental ladies hairdresser, Herr Dietmar Plainer, of Vienna, a leading colourist and stylist...'*

Nevertheless, for other women the search for a new look was yet more radical. A headline in a March edition of the Chronicle revealed, *'Her New Beauty Secret: She Wears a Wig'*. Although the Chronicle's own 'beauty expert' seemed to be some way from converting to the idea, she told her readers, *'Women are buying wigs. Unfortunately, they are not all that comfortable. They make your head rather hot and are inclined to tickle the ears. However, women will suffer for beauty - they've done it before.'*

A hair-do that required constant maintenance with a can of lacquer, one of the new *'gay flowered chiffon blouses'*, two weeks on the Spanish coast, each of these was part of the trappings of modern life in 1963. The memory of the war was fading, the grey austerity of the immediate post war years had been put to one side and good times had come to Essex. Its people meant to enjoy themselves now that their chance had arrived. Nothing was now going to stand between them and their desire to spend, spend, spend.

Wig buying was simply another, albeit unusual, sign of the consumer boom that was beginning to pick up speed in 1963

Essex Chronicle 25th January 1963

At the beginning of the twentieth century steam and the railways it powered represented the very essence of the modern world. But even as early as the 1920s, this pre-eminence was being threatened by the petrol engine and the motor car. By the 1960s, the web of criss-crossed lines which spanned the country, and which had once been the only source of rapid transport over long distances, was now being eclipsed. By the time Dr Richard Beeching put forward his radical plans for the future of Britain's railways, the first motorway had already been opened. Essex, like other counties, was witnessing the ending of its branch line system and the triumph of tarmac over the train...

1964 OH, DR BEECHING!: 'Axe on the rail'

COMMISSIONED BY THE Conservative government of the time, the Beeching closures have developed a terrible reputation amongst those who affectionately remember the picturesque old branch lines with their chugging steam trains and quaint country stations. Beeching has come to be portrayed as if he enacted a sudden bloody massacre, as if he was intent on driving out the very last signs of life from the country's railways. But while it is true that many lines did close as a result of his actions, it should also be said that Beeching did not invent closure. The expansion of local bus services in the inter war period, followed swiftly by the growth in private car ownership, left many rural routes running at a loss. The result was that branch lines had been gradually eroding since their nationalisation in 1947.

Several of Essex's less profitable lines had long since carried their final train. The Kelvedon, Tiptree and Tollesbury Pier Light Railway was just one such route. Its history of expectation and then ignominious failure was common to many other rural lines. The railway was opened in 1904 with hopes that it might bring tourists to Tollesbury and carry the jam from A.C. Wilkin's factory at Tiptree. However, the line was never developed as a success. Holidaymakers failed to arrive, choosing the established resorts of Clacton, Walton and Southend over Tollesbury, while Wilkin's jam could as easily be carried in a fleet of the firm's own motor lorries than by rail. With mounting losses the line finally closed to passengers in 1951 and to freight in 1962. It was a story repeated elsewhere. The line linking Great Yeldham and Haverhill along the Colne Valley, another joining Bishop's Stortford and Braintree, and that between Elsenham and Thaxted suffered similar fates. All saw their rails lifted, sleepers disturbed and small country stations sold off in the years before Beeching was even given a chance to exercise his axe.

WRINGING OF HANDS
Perhaps these early closures should have prepared people for the cuts that Beeching was to bring. But when announced in March 1963, they still met with what the *Essex Chronicle* described as **'...weeping, a gnashing of teeth and much wringing of hands in some quarters...'** Opposition was strongest from Braintree, Saffron Walden, Maldon and Brightlingsea. Beeching's

SEVERAL ESSEX LINES MAY CLOSE

ABOUT 50 Essex railwaymen will be affected by the sweeping proposals for the future of British Railways outlined by Dr. Richard Beeching on Wednesday.

The most important of the Essex proposals are the withdrawal of passenger services on both the Braintree to Witham and Maldon to Witham branch lines.

Other key proposals affecting Essex are:—
- The setting up of a rail head for freight at ...
- Almost certainly high... on suburba...
- Withdraw... servic...

Essex Chronicle 29th March 1963

AXE ON THE RAIL

HERE is weeping, a gnashing of teeth and wringing of hands in some quarters over the proposed closure of certain railway lines and stations in Essex. Arguments for and against can be heard everywhere—and they usually boil down to the same thing. Those likely to be affected are all in favour of the proposals. Those most likely to be hit are strongly in favour of keeping them even though they are run at a thumping great loss. "But this," they argue, "is a sound amenity to the countryside, a calculated loss which must continue." The other taxpayers who constantly dip deeply into their pockets to subsidise these non-paying lines don't see it that way at all.

If, as the result of saving many millions of pounds in the future the level of taxation can be dropped a great many people are going to applaud Dr. Beeching's proposals.

The Essex Chronicle seemed prepared to shed few tears for the passing of rural branch lines

proposals were that each of the towns would see their rail services ended, seemingly marooning them from the wider world. Campaigns were waged to reverse the decisions. For some a case for saving their line rested on arguments that they represented vital amenities for rural towns and villages. For others the railways were things of beauty, a part of a heritage which needed to be protected. **'When the sun shines - glinting on the Colne on one side, and the natural woodland on the other - it is well worth a ride just to stare out of the window...'** read one letter to the local press in defence of the 'Crab and Winkle Line', as the Wivenhoe to Brightlingsea railway had come to be known.

However, the stark truth was that the balance sheets of these lines were showing falling passenger numbers and losses year upon year. For Beeching it was this consideration that mattered and not a railway's wider worth to the community, still less its aesthetic value.

In 1964 the closures began. Only Braintree's link to Witham had been saved, after an appeal to the Ministry of Transport had shown that usage of the line was actually increasing due to the growing numbers of London-bound commuters coming to live in the town. But at Saffron Walden, Brightlingsea and Maldon the same sad scenes were enacted as the day of closure for each line dawned. Station platforms were crowded to wave off those packed upon the last trains. As the last tickets were issued and the last goodbyes said, many speculated that, if only such enthusiasm had been shown before, perhaps the lines might have been saved. But few outside the towns seriously questioned the closures. In fact, the *Chronicle* itself heralded the cuts as a step towards a modern economy: **'If'**, it predicted, **'as a result of saving many millions of pounds in the future the level of taxation can be dropped a great many people are going to applaud Dr Beeching's proposals'**.

CAR CULTURE

Besides, it was the motor car and not the train that was making the main headline news in Essex during that year. Cars were literally everywhere, their numbers having increased in Britain from 1.5 million in 1945 to nearly 9 million in 1964. Their influence was also being felt everywhere. Car accidents, deaths and injuries to pedestrians and cyclists had increased dramatically, so that by the 1960s they appear with an appalling frequency amongst the news pages of the paper. But there was another, brighter side to the car, for it had now become as much an essential accessory to modern living as the television, the refrigerator and the foreign holiday. The *Essex Chronicle* recognised this and provided a weekly motoring column with which to tempt its readers into entering the car culture. This new culture included exciting new models such as the Humber Sceptre, which the column described in glowing terms as **'a** *highly-luxurious and high-speed saloon'*, a car which would *'...appeal as much to the family man and executive looking for comfort at high speeds as it will to any "sporty-minded" motorist'*. For £997 the Sceptre offered the motorist *'virtually everything'* including *'foam rubber individual front seats, a complete heating and ventilation system, screen washers, twin reversing lamps, a clock, a rev counter, padded sun visors, cigarette lighter and built-in safety belts'*.

The car was also busy changing the way Essex looked. 1964 saw the beginning of a fresh phase of road building, with the County Council pledging £17 million towards making the whole length of the A12 into a dual carriage way. In September the newly completed by-pass at Witham was opened by the Minister of Transport, Ernest Marples, with a triumphant prediction that the road represented a *'...further step to speed traffic along the A12 to the coast...'* and that *'No longer will there be the frustrations and delays caused*

The motor age had become well established in the pages of the Essex Chronicle. 18th January 1963

• 109,000 PEOPLE BY 1981

VAST PLANS FOR NEW CHELMSFORD CENTRE

Crime squad starts | **ELECTION KICK-OFF** | **135 MORE SHOPS CAR PARKS FOR 11,200 VEHICLES**

NEWS — COMMENT

AN important report which summarizes about 15 months' work the planning problems of the Central Area of Chelmsford released for publication this week. It has been prepared for Chelmsford Borough Co...

Essex Chronicle 2nd October 1964

by traffic congestion'. Meanwhile more by-passes at Brentwood and Hatfield Peverel were being constructed, while plans were afoot for others at Chelmsford, Boreham and Stanway, along with a motorway linking Bishops Stortford with London. With each of the new road schemes, more and more people were able to travel further and further to work by car. Villages that had once been beyond the reach of the commuter now started to attract people looking for a rural home with pretty country garden and room for that all-important garage.

HOUSEWIFE'S PARADISE

The maps of Essex's towns were also being radically redrawn under the influence of the car. Town planners were beginning to busy themselves, trying to design away the problems of congestion and inadequate parking places. In October 1964 a plan was launched for a new design for Chelmsford. The *Chronicle* called it a *'major surgical operation to the heart of the County Town'*. Its proposals were radical and were to create a design template which other Essex towns soon copied. The scheme included plans for a traffic-free High Street, 135 more shops and the demolition of several much-loved buildings including the town's Corn Exchange. Serving this revamped town centre were to be major new roads and *'car parks for 11,200 vehicles'*. Looking ahead, the *Chronicle* predicted a hopeful future of convenience and easy access, *'It will be a housewife's paradise...No longer will the shopper*

TRAFFIC WARDENS START ON MONDAY

Their object is to be friendly

THE purpose of the ten traffic wardens who will be seen in Chelmsford for the first time on Monday will be to help and guide the motorist rather than prosecute. This is the note of comfort given by police to motorists who have been worried since we announced that the town was to get wardens, some months ago.

The primary function of the traffic wardens will be to help drivers in areas in the town where waiting is restricted or prohibited and by advising dr...... of the parking facilities available.

Prosecutions w... persistent offen... of a po... to...

Essex Chronicle 17th April 1964

have to struggle to the far end of a crowded muddy car park, weighed down with parcels and bulging shopping baskets. A six storey car park will have a passenger exit right into the centre of the new shopping area...The children of today will soon forget the familiar scenes of traffic pile-ups in the High Street, and double-decker buses dominating the scene in the town centre...It [Chelmsford] could become a City - yes, CITY - of great character and one of which we in Essex could all be proud.'

PROBLEMS TO COME

Yet there were signs that the car was bringing problems in its wake, signs too of a growing recognition that it did not lead to freedom for all and that towns would soon have to look to systems with which to control its presence. In April 1964 Colchester and Chelmsford became the first towns in Essex to feel the presence of a new phenomenon. A presence which over the coming years would play a vital role in keeping streets clear and people on the move, yet few would ever have a kind word for them. They were the first Essex traffic wardens. The twenty men appointed included former factory and shop workers, bricklayers, lorry drivers and an ex-Military Policeman. Dressed in their dark uniform with its distinctive yellow-banded hat, the *Chronicle* predicted that the wardens would *'bring enormous benefit'*. Their role was to be one of assisting the public rather than punishing them: *'The purpose of the wardens will be to help and guide the motorist rather than prosecute...to help drivers in areas where waiting is restricted or prohibited and by advising drivers of the parking facilities available...Prosecutions will only be taken against deliberate or persistent offenders'*.

However, the next three decades were to show that the appointment of the first traffic wardens and the building of the first multi-storey car parks, motorways and ring roads could not bring an end to traffic congestion. Alongside their benefits, an ever expanding number of cars brought fresh challenges to the county. As long as more people yearned to have the new Humber Sceptre or the new Triumph Herald parked in their driveway, then the problems would multiply. In the Essex of 1964 the tussle to tame the car was not at its end, but at its very beginning.

Paying to park was hot news in 1964

1964

Amongst the first traffic wardens appointed to the streets of Essex, whose job it was to 'help and guide the motorist', was Ken Sparkes (born 1927). Here he speaks of joining the service in Colchester, the traffic problems that he was expected to solve, issuing tickets and the conflict that sometimes ensued.

TO LISTEN SELECT CD TRACK 7

Even in their earliest days traffic wardens had few friends. Essex Chronicle 24th April 1964

3rd May 1979 saw Britain enter a new era, the era of Thatcherism. The general election showed that Essex people were at the forefront of this shift, as throughout the county many embraced the new blue tide of national politics...

1979 ELECTION: 'the night Essex turned blue'

WHEN A GENERAL election was called in March 1979 by the Labour Prime Minister Jim Callaghan it surprised many, not least the local political parties who had to mobilise local party machines to fight an election in little more than four weeks. At the beginning of campaigns across the county the *Essex Chronicle* stated, perhaps with more optimism than with real expectation, **'all we hope is that between now and polling day the parties rise above the cheap point-scoring behaviour we have seen in the past'**.

Within Essex a set of local issues soon emerged from local meetings and door-step canvassing. Central to these was education and the question of whether the county would be allowed to keep its prestigious grammar schools if a further Labour government committed to comprehensive education were to be returned. Cuts to the NHS were also a hot issue and would remain so in elections for the remainder of the century. Transport dominated too, although calls for alternatives to the car, which were to rise in the 1990s, did not yet hold people's attention. Instead the 'roads protesters' of 1979 were committed to building new ones, with the A12 by-pass of Chelmsford and the M25 'London Orbital' being top of their list.

But for many the election was won and lost through a set of other issues that were dominating the country. In the months preceding the election the Labour Government had implemented its 'incomes policy' which aimed to control growing inflation by limiting wage increases. At the same time unemployment figures had risen to levels not seen since before World War Two with 1.2 million people now out of work. From the roots of these problems came what quickly became known as the 'Winter of Discontent'. The result was industrial chaos across Britain as Trade Unions mobilised support for their wage demands through strike action and by working to rule.

Essex Chronicle 30th March 1979

CHAOS DAY

The Winter of Discontent brought industrial problems to Essex that came close to those of the General Strike of 1926 (see chapter six). The culmination of the struggle came in a day of action organised by local unions in January 1979. The *Essex Chronicle* primed its readers in advance, warning them of what it called:

'MOAN-DAY MONDAY! - next Monday will be the biggest ever chaos day for thousands of Essex people as various trade unions are to call out hundreds of key manual workers on a one-day strike...schools will close, hospital services will be severely curtailed, roads ungritted, council parks closed, libraries shut, ambulance staff attending emergency calls only, hospital wards remaining uncleaned and household dustbins unemptied'.

The day of decision for Marconi

OVER 1,000 manual workers at Marconi Communications will come into work this morning to find out if they are to resume normal working — or stop work altogether.

For the industrial dispute that has troubled the company's factories for the last two weeks has finally come to a head.

An improved offer has been made by the management this week but the results of a secret ballot of union members will decide whether it is accepted or rejected.

And they won't discover their fate until this morning when the shop stewards have counted up the votes of the 1,200 members.

"Only four of the seven union demands have been answered," said Works Convener, Mr. David Pearce. But he refused to be drawn into predicting the likely outcome. "It is up to the individual members to decide whether the three points neglected by the management are important.

"But we are hopeful to get back to normal working as soon as possible — if the offer is accepted."

A lightning strike by Marconi Communications shop floor workers stunned the company last Thursday and since then intensive talks have been going on in an attempt to end the dispute.

And it was at a meeting between management and unions on Monday afternoon that the improved offer was made.

Pay rises have been promised, as have improved holidays for long serving employees.

Shop stewards from the Amalgamated Engineering Union met on Tuesday and decided to put the offer to their membership.

And they were meeting again last night until late into the evening discussing the results of the ballot held on Wednesday and Thursday.

They will be deciding on a course of action but their members who have already decided the outcome will not find out until they arrive at work this morning whether they will be staying there — or starting an all out official strike.

Murder charge

MR. TERENCE HALL, 33, unemployed factory worker, of Meadway, Maldon, was remanded in custody by the town's magistrates on Monday afternoon, charged with the murder of three of his daughters, Tracey (11), Sharon (9) and Amanda (7).

He is due to appear again next Wednesday.

A walk out at Britvic

The factory gate meeting at Britvic on Wednesday morning.

PRODUCTION lines came to a standstill at Chelmsford's Britvic factory on Wednesday, when nearly 500 workers — protesting about old waste food they claimed had been left in their canteen — staged a one-day wild-cat...

Essex Chronicle 6th April 1979

Teachers action hits schools
HUNDREDS SENT HOME

Essex Chronicle 4th May 1979

Even the newspaper and its circulation was hit as lorry drivers refused to transport vital newsprint to Chelmsford.

Problems rumbled on into the election campaign. In April there were disputes at Marconi's and Britvic's plants in Chelmsford, while in May 500 teachers from around the county called a half-day strike as hundreds of children were sent home in what the *Essex Chronicle* condemned as **'a sad and tragic act'**. In the face of this the Conservative Party of Mrs Thatcher held increasing appeal. It promised a new approach to government which castigated what it saw as the inefficiency of the Welfare State, its bureaucracy and the dependency that it was thought to create. In its place Thatcherism promoted the values of self-reliance, independence and enterprise.

NECK-AND-NECK

The message seemed to strike a chord amongst Essex people. In Chelmsford the vote saw the Conservative Norman St. John-Stevas returned for the sixth consecutive time, but only after what the *Essex Chronicle* described as **'a neck-and-neck tussle with local "boy" Stuart Mole'**. The Chelmsford vote had also been notable for **'a sensational official boob'** in which 1,300 votes had to be discarded after they had been marked wrongly by officials. Elsewhere Tory victories were described as **'overwhelming'** in Braintree and Colchester, while they were said to have **'romped home'** in Brentwood, Saffron Walden and Maldon. But it was Basildon that had started not only the county's but also the nation's slide towards Conservatism on that election night. Up until that time the town had been a secure Labour seat, but now it turned blue as the Conservatives enacted **'a shock election win as they swept to victory with an 11 per cent swing'**. The victor was a young company secretary named Harvey Proctor.

The outcome of the 1979 election thrust Essex into the political spotlight. Over the coming years 'Basildon Man', 'Essex Man' and 'Essex Woman' were to become shorthand terms used by the nation's media when it wanted to portray a stereotype of the new, brash breed of Tory voter. Skilled working-class or lower middle-class, affluent, young, a house owner, car driver, perhaps taking holidays in Florida, this was a breed of Tory for whom Essex was viewed as the natural home. It was to be a long-standing stereotype, one that endured three more Conservative election victories and two Prime Ministers in Margaret Thatcher and John Major.

That was the time when...

The *Essex Chronicle* carried an advertisement for the 'Asagnor' dining table with its *'restrained and elegant look'*. Available from Bolingbroke and Wenley for just £186. Meanwhile Pussycat Boutique of Ingatestone was advertising bikinis at £6.99, dresses from £8.99 and cheese cloth shirts at £7.99.

House prices seem modest by today's standards. For £19,250 it was possible to buy a 3 bedroom, detached house in Springfield, Chelmsford. The house concerned promised buyers an *'immaculate'* interior including a *'Pampas coloured suite'*.

But wages were also lower; in the jobs columns of the paper a Brentwood stockbrokers advertises for a new post of *'Data Terminal Operator'* offering the inducements of an annual salary of £2,500 plus daily luncheon vouchers of 40p.

The Chronicle liked to make much of the youthfulness of Chelmsford's Liberal candidate, Stuart Mole. He was to go on to lose at two more General Elections after 1979

Election day saw the Conservatives sweep the board in Essex

1979

Stuart Mole (born 1949) came to Chelmsford in 1970. Over the coming years he helped to revitalise the Liberal Party's standing in the town. In 1972 he stood successfully as a candidate for Chelmsford Borough Council. However, from 1974 through to 1987 he stood unsuccessfully as a parliamentary candidate for the seat of Chelmsford in five elections. Here he recalls his early days as a councillor, the two very close election defeats of 1974, the campaign and election night of 1979 and the relationship between the press and politicians.
TO LISTEN SELECT CD TRACK 8

Across the county cinemas were showing the latest releases which included *'Julia'*, an A-certificate starring Jane Fonda and Vanessa Redgrave, and *'The Deer Hunter'* certificate X.

A stir was created in Chelmsford where the Civic Theatre was opening its doors with **'The Boys in the Band'**, which the *Essex Chronicle* described as **'one of the most controversial plays ever to be staged in the town, with the main characters homosexuals and the language strong in several somewhat explicit scenes'**.

Staying in on a Saturday promised a night of TV entertainment on BBC 1 which included *'Rolf on Saturday OK'*, *'Dad's Army'*, *'The Val Doonican Music Show'*, *'The Rockford Files'* and *'Match of the Day'*.

In sport Essex County Cricket Club were about to begin the 1979 season and, unbeknown to them and their supporters, the most successful era in the club's history. A cricket team that up until then had been notable for the style of their play but for an overall failure to achieve, was to win two trophies that season. Writing in his 'exclusive' column for the *Chronicle*, Essex captain Keith Fletcher seems to have been blessed with foresight: **'To achieve anything, you have to have team unity and players in the side with the ability to pop-up with a match-winning performance. I fancy that we have such qualities in the present Essex squad.'**

In comparison with the tornadoes, floods, hurricanes, earthquakes and volcanic eruptions which befall other parts of the world, it seems churlish to talk of 'natural disasters' in the context of Essex. The county is one in which the natural world rarely threatens anything more challenging than a frost covered car windscreen or the potential for sunburn to pale arms and legs. But perhaps it is because of this benign relationship with nature that, when we are presented with anything out of the ordinary, it comes as such a surprise. So it was then that the high winds and damage to property of an October night in 1987 came quickly to be known as 'the night of the Great Storm'...

1987 THE GREAT STORM: 'as if a giant had strode across the land'

DAVE SMITH HAD had a difficult few months. As the *Essex Chronicle*'s weatherman he had already failed to predict a torrential downpour in August which brought flooding to Chelmsford. He had also failed to foresee a similar cloudburst which swamped villages around Braintree and Maldon in the autumn. Now on Thursday 15 October 1987 he filed his latest weekly forecast to the newspaper. It read: **'More wet weather on the way...with blustery showers and sunny spells'**. But Dave Smith was again wide of the mark, for those **'blustery showers'** materialised in the form of winds that topped 100 mph and which brought widespread devastation. This was the night when Essex witnessed the full force of **'the hurricane'**.

Thankfully the storm arrived at night, reaching its peak in the early hours of Friday morning. Coming without a warning, the winds might have caused a human tragedy on a scale not seen since the floods of 1953 if they had struck crowded daytime roads and streets. As it was, no one in the county lost their life, although several people had lucky escapes. Many others actually slept through the storm and awoke with amazed eyes the next morning. The *Chronicle* described the scene that confronted them: **'...it was as if a giant had strode across the land, tearing up mighty oaks and squashing human endeavour in its path...Several million pounds worth of damage affected almost every corner of the county...There wasn't a street or a coppice that completely escaped the hurricane as it blasted trees, brick walls, roofs, caravans and greenhouses like matchwood'**.

THE DAMAGE
The aftermath of the storm took time to remedy. Roads were blocked by fallen trees. The trains initially faced similar obstacles and then a more familiar foe **'in the shape of leaves on the line'** which created **'operating difficulties'** into

1987 THE GREAT STORM 73

Mr Nick Saunders, from Baddow House, Great Baddow, sitting on the giant cedar tree which smashed builders' huts and a garage in Great Baddow.

Storm damage at Great Baddow

Emergency plan in operation

CHELMSFORD Borough Council's peacetime emergency plan was brought into operation... were wrecked in the storm. A man who lived in a shed in Boreham has also been re-housed by the council. Many council houses had extensive roof damage and chimney stacks... the circumstances." Parks in Chelmsford were devastated. Over 500 large mature specimen trees were uprooted and twice... from damaged trees, and w be closed for at least anoth week.

the following days. Three hundred of the county's seven hundred schools were forced to close while damage was repaired. The worst hit had been Chelmsford's John Payne School *'where the roof had been ripped off'*. Here as in many other cases the bill for the storm was to fall to Essex County Council, who announced that their insurance would not cover the estimated £8 million cost. Without the prospect of help from central government a council spokesman glumly confirmed *'We do not insure against tempest although we are insured against fire. Very few authorities insure against tempest'*. Meanwhile British Telecom was busy working around the clock replacing six hundred miles of telephone cable across the region, along with electricity engineers who were trying to restore power to thousands of homes.

COWBOY BUILDERS

For the less scrupulous the storm offered an opportunity to make money. Within days Essex police were warning the public to be aware of 'cowboy builders' with reports of *'pick up trucks wandering around the county purporting to be roofers or tilers...it is very easy for anybody with just a scant knowledge of roofing to jump on the bandwagon'*. Letters to the *Chronicle* complained of builders who were *'charging £50 to replace a roof tile'* and who were making *'£600 for one day's work charging exorbitant rates, with their call out charges, parts and VAT'*.

But the storm's opportunities did not end with the building trade. For many people it seemed to give a fleeting chance to return to a time when neighbours helped each other and neighbourhoods were enthused with the 'Dunkirk

Essex Chronicle 30th October 1987

spirit' of old. *'It was marvellous how the community responded to the havoc'*, reported the Chronicle. *'Neighbours who seldom speak to each other suddenly became allies, battling to save dangerous garage roofs, tying down greenhouses and giving shelter to those whose homes were threatened with danger'*. As one Roxwell inhabitant told the paper, *'We hadn't spoken to our neighbours for twenty years because we just don't see them - now we have got to know them and their names. So at least the storms have had one good effect in bringing people together'*.

For families too, one of the most profound and lasting influences of the storm was a taste of home life as it might have been in times before electricity and its world of microwave meals, central heating, radio and television. In the days after the storm, to find out how a typical Essex household was coping the Chronicle visited the Carlile family in their Chelmsford home:

'Cooking on camping stoves and open fires has become a way of life for hundreds of residents days after the hurricane brought down power lines..."I suppose you could say we are getting used to a very rustic way of life, burning logs in our fire place so we can have hot water for baths and washing", said Mrs Carlile. "Cooking meals is a bit more tricky, lots of fry ups by candlelight! It gets quite homely at night with candles to light us to bed." said Mr Carlile'.

HUGE TREES LOST

But the biggest impact of the storm, the one that seemed to preoccupy most people's thoughts, was not a human story. Instead it related to the county's trees. Here the loss was expressed in traumatic tones. *'Trees that have stood for many years resisting all manner of winter storms finally succumbed'*, reported the Chronicle, *'Huge trees, some hundreds of years old and seemingly immovable were lost. The skyline of many areas will never be the same again.'* Parks in and around Chelmsford were said to have been devastated. *'Over five hundred large mature trees were uprooted and twice as many have been severely damaged and will have to be felled. It is feared that up to 2,000 trees will eventually be lost'*.

Muddling through: at home with the Carlile family in Chelmsford

Essex Chronicle 30th October 1987

Mr Mike Lambert surveys the damage done to one of his sheds after Thursday night's force 12 winds. Three of the seven sheds on Spring Elms Farm, Little Baddow, were destroyed by the hurricane-force gale. This shed was home to 6,000 chickens, but the fierce winds razed the building, leaving 1,500 chickens dead. Mr Lambert and his neighbours were able to save the rest. It was the only shed with livestock in it. Mr Lambert said: "The neighbours were fantastic and the insurance company have been terrific, they have been along already. But there was £60,000 worth of damage approximately."

Tree damage like this photographed at Highwood seemed dramatic. However, the long term implications were often positive

Undeterred by the wrecked stand around them, a few Chelmsford City fans watch their side days after the storm

In the weeks and months that followed came a mania for clearing-up and replenishment. In every town and in every village the sight of fallen trees was quickly followed by the sound of chainsaws. The mood was one of profound loss, with fallen trees mourned as if they had been well-loved relatives or faithful friends. But underlying this loss was a determination that the landscape should be restored. The aftermath also witnessed a host of money raising and tree planting schemes. Nowhere was this impulse better illustrated than in the example of a Bicknacre man, Mr Alan Goodwin, who in the week after the storm won £235,000 on the football pools. Posing for the obligatory press photograph receiving his winner's cheque from a 'page-three' model, he was asked what would be his first purchase with the money. Would it be a new car? A new house? A holiday for the family? In answering Mr Goodwin captured the county's mood when he declared that he **'would like to buy a large oak tree for the village green'**, explaining that **'we lost so many in the storms'**.

However, even in those first few weeks after the storm, there were doubting voices raised against the urge to rebuild the landscape. Amongst the articles and the letters pages of the *Essex Chronicle* came those who argued that the

With the storm came transport chaos (above) and countless episodes of damage to property (below)

storm had been an act of nature, a natural culling, and that natural restoration of woodland would occur in its own time. The Essex Naturalist Trust put forward one of the most vociferous cases, arguing that little or no action was often better than too much: **'We have to carefully decide on the future management of habitats that have taken so many hundreds of years to develop'**, said a spokesman. **'Tree planting may well not be appropriate, as some of these woodlands will regenerate of their own accord'**.

The Great Storm had not only been a story of loss. For every tree that had fallen, a new habitat had been created. In the places where trees had once stood, sunlight now flooded in, giving fresh plants and replacement saplings the chance to take root. As the bulk of each toppled tree began to decay, so then animals and insects also found new homes and new food sources. As the weeks and months passed, a landscape which many thought had been destroyed simply passed on to a fresh phase in its evolution.

That was the time when...

The *Essex Chronicle* was also evolving with the times. Its 'Mrs Chelmsford' competition was some way removed from the standard beauty contests run in the past. The role of the winner, Mrs Christine Playford, was one of do-gooder rather than decoration as each week the *Chronicle* pictured her upon her tireless round of opening functions, fetes and visiting old people's centres.

The *Chronicle* also had its own 'agony aunt' dedicated to the problems of its teenage readers. Amongst her weekly letters came one from a mother concerned about her lonely son, a sailor in the Royal Navy. Appealing to **'all nice girls'** to write to her son, she described him in tempting terms as **'very trendy in his dress, with a sense of humour'**.

For those seeking an evening out in Essex, there was an enviable list of possibilities which included films such as 'Full Metal Jacket', 'Superman' and 'Hellraiser', concerts from 'Chas and Dave' and 'The Baron Knights', and wrestling with a bill at the Chancellor Hall, Chelmsford, which contained 'Bone Crusher Barret', 'Bully Boy Muir' and 'Cry Baby Jimmy Breaks'.

1987 THE GREAT STORM

Meet two unsung heroes of the hurricane — Len Poulton (left) and Peter Fox, who are British Telecom 'woodpeckers'. Their task is to check out BT's 42,000 Southend area telephone poles, tapping and digging to test them for rot. Without this regular testing many more poles would have been blown down in the high winds. Peter, from Chelmsford, said: "The only way to tell if a pole may be rotten is to tap it with a hammer. If it sounds amiss then we push a sharp spike into the wood to see how bad things are." Len and Peter have now been transferred to the repair and maintenance unit until the emergency is over.

For anyone fearing over-excitement at these tempting prospects, there was the option of an evening in front of the TV. Here Saturday night contained such highlights as ''Allo, 'Allo', 'The Russ Abbot Show', 'Bob's Full House' and 'Miami Vice'.

Essex Chronicle 23rd October 1987

1987

The devastation of the Great Storm appeared to many Essex people to have destroyed a much loved landscape. But for Janet Spencer (born 1962) and Peter Smith (born 1927) the storm offered hope and opportunity. At the time both were working to preserve the county's woodland, Janet with the Nature Conservancy Council and Peter with the Essex Naturalist Trust. Here they discuss their first reactions to the storm, the huge clearing up process that entailed, the benefits of storm damage to the woodland environment and their thoughts on the present challenges faced by the Essex landscape.
TO LISTEN SELECT CD TRACK 9

WIND BILL TOPS £9m

IT WILL cost Essex County Council about £8 million to repair damage to buildings caused by the storm of two weeks' ago — and the immediate emergency clearing up cost amount to another £1 million.

The news was given to Tuesday's full meeting of the county council by co-ordinating and finance committee chairman, Cllr Paul White.

And he added that it did not look as though the council was going to receive any financial help from the Government towards the cost.

He told councillors, "I am

"Since the level of a penny rate in Essex is £2.4 million it seems clear that the Government's emergency arrangements will not apply to the Essex circumstances and that our expenditure will be met out of our emergency fund in the normal way.

"As the cost of the future works required to restore

By Kathleen Corby

This was the scene at St John Payne School in Patching Hall Lane on Wednesday as workmen got down t

Putting the lid bac on at St John Payn

This chronicle of Essex's recent history ends, as it began, with a royal story. People awoke on Sunday 31st August 1997 to the news that Diana, Princess of Wales, had been killed in a car accident during the early hours of the morning. The news spread rapidly. Within one or two hours the crash was dominating media headlines around the world, a position it was to hold for days to come. This was predictable, for if nothing else Diana had led a life whose last years were embroiled in controversy. A predicament upon which many editors and broadcasters were only too happy to feed and add to. Looking back now what seems so striking and altogether less predictable was the public response to the death. The loss of Diana seemed to hold personal significance for so many people. The result was a period of public mourning and commemoration unlike any other in the county's history...

1997 THE DEATH OF DIANA: 'beautiful, flawless, like a porcelain doll'

Lighting candles for Diana, Chelmsford Cathedral

COMING FIVE DAYS after the crash the *Essex Chronicle*'s edition of the 4th September was too late to do justice to the initial stunned responses of people around the county. Besides, the shocking news had already been picked over again and again by television, radio and the daily papers. So instead the *Chronicle* drew its focus from the great tide of public reactions which had been building all week, for in the days which followed the accident it seemed as if almost everyone wanted to pay some tribute to the Princess.

Some acts of commemoration were official, well organised, the result of emergency meetings and sudden dictates from 'above'. Across the county Union flags flew at half-mast on office buildings, town halls and churches. At the hour of the funeral itself shops shut, buses pulled to the side of roads to observe two minutes' silence, a convention also observed at the county's railway stations. Extreme events called for extreme measures. Some couples postponed weddings which had been fixed long ago for that fateful Saturday. Others went ahead but only with the promise that **'a minute's silence would be incorporated into the ceremonies'**. Essex was reported to be at a **'virtual halt...streets deserted'** during the service itself, with people gathered inside watching on television or else having left for London to try and gain a brief glimpse of the passing cortege.

Many acts of commemoration took on simpler, more spontaneous forms. By the Monday after the accident, remembrance books had been opened in every town and in many villages across the county. Situated in civic halls, places of worship, even supermarkets, the books drew queues of people, some

COUNTY MOURNS DIANA

Essex Chronicle 5th September 1997

There was a special poignancy to the news for the very few Essex people who had met Diana

The county pays tribute
Such a beacon of kindness, love and hope ...

Essex Chronicle 5th September 1997

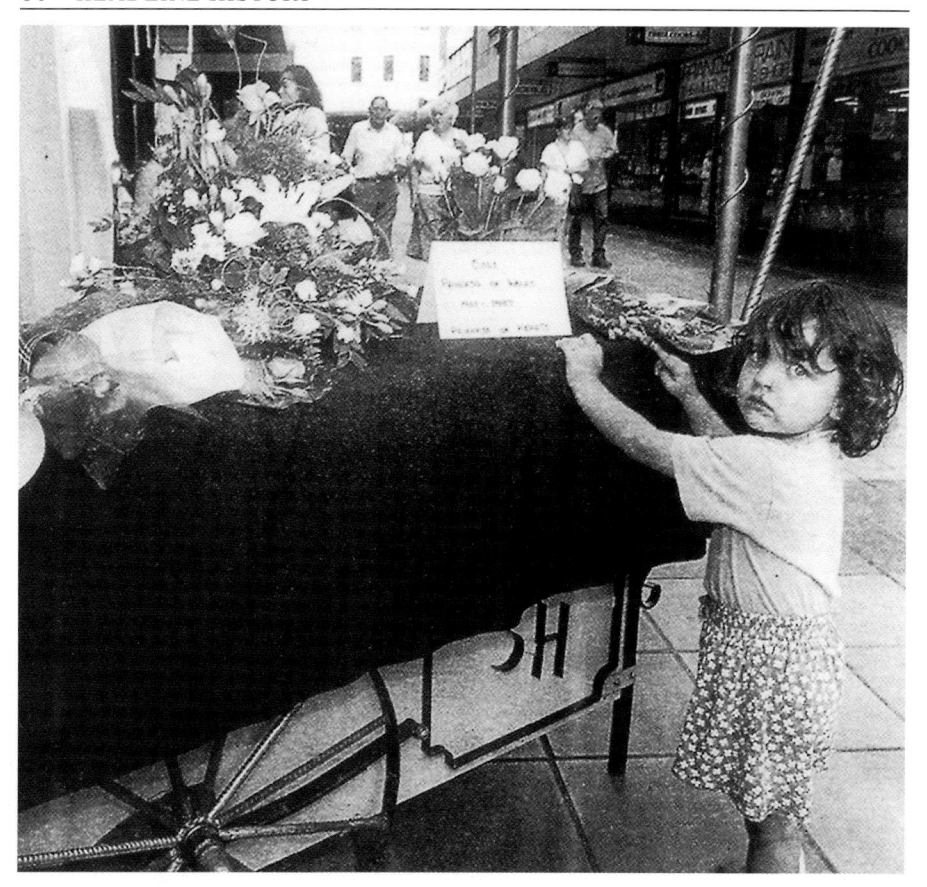

Diana's death triggered a succession of floral tributes around the county

leaving nothing more than a line and a signature, others filling several pages with their thoughts. People also took to laying flowers as a way of paying tribute. Without prior organisation and without official participation, places became sites of floral tribute. Some were obvious choices, war memorials being a particularly favoured location. But elsewhere, a spontaneous act by one person often led others to follow. In Chelmsford, for example, market trader Swaley Howell had decided to **'deck his traditional barrow in black velvet when he opened for business early on Tuesday morning, and place a simple floral display with a hand-written reference to the Princess. During the day passers-by placed flowers on the barrow as it slowly became recognised as a focal point of the townspeople's grief and respect.'**

PUBLIC AND PRESS

The uniformity of the public reaction to Diana's death was startling. In the weeks that followed, the *Chronicle* reported no breaks in the reverence shown towards her, no dissenting voices, no signs that people thought the public and press reaction had gone too far. If there were opposing voices then they were quiet or had been quietened. Rarely can the events in one individual's life have had so much influence on Essex. A fact made even more remarkable by the absence of any significant link between Diana and the county.

The attraction of Diana to Essex people, as with people everywhere, was built on different foundations. Propagated on newspaper front-pages, the covers of glossy magazines and television 'specials', her image as a beautiful young wife and mother, allied to the belief that she was approachable and 'human' gave her unique appeal. Diana was part of the royal family and yet portrayed herself in a style that no member of that family had ever managed. If the reaction in Essex to the death of Diana is compared with that which greeted the death of Queen Victoria in 1901 (see chapter two), we see sadness and the desire to mourn in both events. Yet there are also startling differences. Victoria's commemoration contained an air of distance and formality, attitudes which reflected the relationship then between crown and people. The nation had lost its figure-head, and for that there was great sadness. But the Queen's own life was something people knew less about and had less emotional attachment to. But with Diana the loss appeared more personal. Some individuals mourned as if she had been a close friend, even a sister or mother. After all, the public seemed to know of virtually every detail of her life, even down to details of a sad marriage and subsequent love affairs. A great deal had changed in the twentieth century, and the ever shrinking private lives of the royal family was just one sign of this.

DOOMED AND TORMENTED

In the weeks that followed the funeral, the *Essex Chronicle* contained many eulogies to Diana, all reflecting this personal connection. *'Beautiful, flawless, like a porcelain doll'* was how one woman expressed her own view of the Princess, *'I just couldn't believe it. I watched the television in shock and burst into tears'*. The *Chronicle*'s own assistant editor, John Hill, wrote of his reaction to the death. In a highly personal column he struggled to explain why he and his family had felt they must make the pilgrimage to Kensington Palace to lay flowers at Diana's former home:

'It is not easy to define why - we just felt drawn as a family. And we will be at tomorrow's funeral for the same reason. May be it was a diversion from the day-long feeling of welling tears for the end of a doomed and tormented life; may be we rediscovered just how much we love our country...may be it was just to cleanse our souls from the shame of being human beings, of being associated by species with those vultures who took photographs of Diana as she lay dying in the wreckage of that dreadful car crash. Whatever the reason, we laid our flowers in the gathering gloom with my daughter's simple message: Diana, with love.'

The Chronicle liked to remember Diana in happier times

Hill's comments sum up much of the feeling that surrounded Diana's death; few Essex people had ever met her, and yet many felt as if they had known her.

SIGNS OF FRACTURE

The events of that August weekend also highlighted one final feature about life in Essex at the close of the twentieth century. This was that the public face of reverence and respect for the monarchy was beginning to show signs of fracture. This is not to say that the county became a hotbed of republicanism with the death of Diana, but it did signal a shift in opinion regarding the royal family. The image of Diana as *'simply an angel, a saint'* cast a shadow of doubt over the conduct and the standing of the monarchy. *'A wronged woman hounded to the end...she will be forever young'* was the message that Hill had for readers. *'Despite the misery of a life lived in the public glare with a husband who loved someone else, she lit the world with vibrancy and colour...The royals took away her right to be known as her Royal Highness, but she remained the People's Princess. And history will show that that was a more important title by far.'*

This represented a language and a sentiment unmentionable just twenty, or perhaps even ten, years previously. The reverence and the unquestioned loyalty that the newspaper had always presented was showing signs of reformation. But in doing this, the *Essex Chronicle*, which had for so long charted the county's changing tastes, emotions, aspirations and opinions, was simply documenting the latest of the sea changes in the thinking of the county's people. A new century and a new millennium awaited their next move.

In the absence of any place of direct connection to Diana people turned to other public sites of remembrance. Here messages and flowers cover Colchester's war memorial

INDEX

People, places and organisations

Albert, Prince: 1
America, North: 6, 31
Arsenal Football Club: 41
Ashdon: 13-6
Australia: 6, 58

Baddow, Great: 1, 4
Baldwin, Stanley: 25
Banbury Town Football Club: 41
Bardfield, Great: 54
Barnard, Mr: 32
Baron Knights, The: 76
Barret, Bonecrusher: 76
Basildon: 69-70
Beeching, Dr Richard: 63-4
Berlin: 36
Bicknacre: 75
Billericay: 2, 27, 58
Birdbrook: 13-4, 16
Bishops Stortford: 21, 63, 66
Blackpool Town Football Club: 41, 43-5
Boers: 5
Bolingbroke and Wenley: 7, 70
Boreham: 54, 66
Bow: 24
Bradford City Football Club: 42-3
Braintree: 3, 23, 24, 26, 32, 54, 57, 63-4, 72
Breaks, Cry-Baby Jimmy: 76
Brentwood: 2, 7, 17, 24, 66, 69, 70
Brightlingsea: 4, 63, 64
Britain: 1, 5, 6, 16, 21, 23, 31, 38, 52, 54, 59, 60, 63, 64, 68
British Broadcasting Corporation (BBC): 26, 71
British Buses: 38
British Telecom: 73
Britvic Ltd: 69
Brown, John: 1
Browne, Frederick: 27-30
Bumpstead, Helions: 13-6
Bumpstead, Steeple: 2, 13-6
Burnham-on-Crouch: 2, 46
Burton, P.C.: 15
Butlin, Billy: 61

Calais: 22
Calcutta: 22
Callaghan, James: 68

Cambridge: 19, 34
Cambridgeshire: 13, 15
Camps, Castle: 15
Canvey Island: 46, 48-51, 54
Carlile, Mr and Mrs: 74
Channel Islands: 60
Charles, Prince: 57
Chas and Dave: 76
Chelmsford: 4, 7, 9, 11, 12, 19, 24-5, 33-4, 39, 46, 57, 62, 66-7, 68-70, 71, 74, 80
Chelmsford Area Planning Group: 39
Chelmsford City Football Club: 41
Chelmsford, Bishop of: 15
Churchill, Winston: 25
Civil Defence: 58
Clacton-on-Sea: 24, 46
Coggeshall: 3
Colchester: 3, 8, 9, 19, 21, 24, 33, 43, 44, 57, 67, 69
Colchester United Football Club: 41-5
Colchester, Bishop of: 5
Colne Valley: 63
Colne, The: 64
Conservative Party: 25, 63, 65, 68-70
Cosmos Ltd: 60
Costa Brava: 60
County of London Electric Supply Co: 38
Crittall Ltd: 23
Cromer: 9
Crowe and Co. Ltd: 7

Daily Herald: 12
Daily Mail: 12
Danbury: 2
Darwin, Charles: 21
Diana, Princess: 57, 78-82
Doherty, Peter: 42
Doole, Joe: 11
Dover: 22
Dovercourt: 32
Drysdale, Mr L: 19
Dunkirk: 36, 50
Dunmow, Great: 6

Edgar, Percy: 26
Edward, Dr: 10
Elizabeth II, Queen: 52-7
Elsenham: 63
England: 13, 16, 25, 31, 36, 37, 57, 59
Epping: 19, 20, 24

Essex Constabulary: 24
Essex County Council: 22, 73
Essex County Cricket Club: 71
Essex Farmers' Union: 41
Essex Naturalists' Trust: 76
Essex Record Office: 20
Essex Rivers Board: 48
Europe: 6, 16, 32, 59-60
Everest, Mount: 54

Fambridge, North: 57
Faulkbourne: 57
Faulkner, Mr: 10
Felixstowe: 46
Fenton, Mrs: 44-5
Fenton, Ted: 44-5
Fletcher, Keith: 71
Florida: 70
Forward, Kickett: 8
Foulness: 51
France: 2, 20, 24
Frinton-on-Sea: 42

Galleywood: 1
Gatey, P.C.: 15
George VI, King: 52
Germany: 16, 22, 24, 35, 38
Gimson, Dr: 10
God: 5, 20, 39, 53
Goodwin, Alan: 75
Gray, Isobel: 26
Grays: 24
Great Eastern Railway: 9, 12
Greece: 60
Gutteridge, Mrs: 30
Gutteridge, P.C.: 27-30

Halstead: 1, 3, 6
Ham, East: 21
Ham, West: 21, 48
Ham, West United Football Club: 41
Handley, Mr R.A.F.: 42
Harlow: 57
Harwich: 6, 24, 32, 33, 46-8
Hatfield Peverel: 66
Haverhill: 63
Hedingham, Sible: 57
Hicks, Mr: 8
Hill, John: 81-2
Horton Ices: 8
House of Commons: 13
Howell, Swaley: 80
Huddersfield Town Football Club: 42, 45

Huntley and Palmer Ltd: 38

Ilford: 19, 21, 25
Inde Coope Ltd: 24
Independent Labour Party: 6
India: 22, 52-3
Ingatestone: 70
Ireland: 6
Isle of Wight: 6

Jaywick: 49-51
John Payne School, Chelmsford: 73

Karl, Dr: 10
Kelvedon: 4, 63
Kennedy, Mrs: 30
Kennedy, William: 27-30
Kensington Palace: 81
Kodak Ltd: 17

Labour Party: 68
Lansbury, George: 15
Leach, Fred: 48
Leyton: 21
Liverpool Street Station, London: 9, 10, 24, 28
London: 10, 12, 19, 22, 24, 33, 38, 66, 78
London and North-Eastern Railway: 24
Lovell, Dr: 28
Lowestoft Town Football Club: 45

Major, John: 70
Majorca: 60
Maldon: 4, 6, 24, 33, 46-7, 63-4, 69, 72
Manchester United Football Club: 41
Manningtree: 48
Mansfield, Private H.: 22
Maples, Ernest: 65
Marconi: 24, 59, 69
Margeretting: 40
Matthews, Stanley: viii, 45
Mersea Island: 46
Metropolitan Police: 13, 15, 28
Ministry of Food: 54
Ministry of Information: 37
Mole, Stuart: 69
Mortensen, Stan: 45
Muir, Bully Boy: 76

Napoleon: 24
National Agricultural Labourers' and Rural Workers' Union: 13

National Health Service: 18, 68
Navy, Army and Air Force Institutes (NAAFI): 37
Nepal: 54
New Zealand: 54
Newport: 22
Norfolk: 9, 12
Norwich: 24
Notley, Black: 54

Ongar 4, 40, 57
Orkney 2
Orwell, The 46

Pankhurst, Sylvia: 15
Paris: 11
Pentonville Prison: 30
Pepper, P.C.: 38
Pest Control Ltd: 58
Pickfords Ltd: 60
Plainer, Dietmar: 62
Playford, Christine: 76
Pleshey: 2
Proctor, Harvey: 69
Pussycat Boutique: 70

Rhine, The: 36
Ridgewell: 14-5
Romford: 19, 24
Romford, Bishop of: 29, 35
Roxwell: 74
Royal Navy: 76
Ruffle, Richard: 13-4

Saffron Walden: 15, 20, 24, 63-4, 70
Savoy Orpheans: 26
Scotland: 31
Scotland Yard: 28
Smart Brothers: 17
Smith, David: 72
South Africa: 5
South Woodham Ferrers: 38, 58
Southend-on-Sea: 19, 24, 33, 39, 46, 60, 61
Spain: 62
Spalding, Fred: 9, 12
Springfield: 70
St. John Stevas, Norman: 69
St. Paul's Cathedral: 1
Standard Ironworks: 24
Stanford Rivers: 3
Stanford-le-Hope: 25
Stanway: 66
Stapleford Abbots: 27
Stopes, Dr Marie: 26
Stour, The: 46
Stratford: 17
Strupar, William: vii

Sturmer: 14-5
Suez Canal: viii
Suffolk: 11, 13, 15

Tasmania: 17
Thames Haven: 25
Thatcher, Margaret: 69, 70
Thaxted: 63
Thomas Cook Ltd: 60
Thresh, Dr J.C.: 19
Tilbury: 24, 48, 51
Tillingham: 6
Tiptree: 57, 63
Tollesbury: 2-3, 63
Trades Union Congress: 23

United States of America: viii
Upminster: 48

Victoria, Queen: viii, 1-4, 5-7, 54, 81
Vienna: 62

Wales: 31, 38
Wall Street: 31
Wallasea: 51
Waltham Cross: 19
Walthamstow: 21, 33
Walton-on-the-Naze: 47, 61
Wandsworth Prison: 30
Warley: 30
Waterloo, Battle of: viii
West Country, The: 61
West Ham United Football Club: 41, 44
West Wickham: 15
Westminster Abbey: 56
Weston Colville: 15
Wethersfield: 54
Wickford: 3
Wilkin, A.C.: 63
Wimbish: 13, 19
Witham: 3, 6-7, 9-12, 19, 33, 64
Withersfield: 15
Wivenhoe: 46, 64
Woolwich: 29
Wrexham United Football Club: 41

Yeldham, Great: 63